A wonderfully approachable book about lean, Ken's deep experience at To[illegible] in healthcare coupled with his obvious respect for the management system shines through in his storytelling. Leaders will find Lean Leadership on a Napkin *to be informative as well as practical, leaving the reader wanting to learn and apply their newfound knowledge.*

— Craig Vercruysse, Former Executive. Sutter Health

Ken and I met five years ago when my team interviewed him to join our Strategic and Organizational Transformation Department at Providence Little Company of Mary Medical Center. His clearly impressive accomplishments co-creating the Sutter Improvement System, the University of Toyota, and the many organizational development achievements in between spoke for themselves, but the moment he conversed with us, the moment that first napkin scribble was shared, we were all hooked.

Ken, in his typical humble and gentle nature, slid right into the mix of our blossoming team, generously eager to connect and serve—respectfully meeting us where we were at in our Lean journey. During our few years of formally working together, Ken graciously coached, taught, and mentored our team, which catapulted many of us to dive passionately into the world of Lean leadership. In parallel, he quickly made a profound impact on the organization's culture via development of his Managing for Daily Improvement curriculum, that he taught with passion and humor to hundreds of caregivers. He empowered these leaders at all levels to identify, execute, and sustain improvement work and successfully moved the needle in caregiver engagement through his famous sessions on Kata Coaching.

Somewhere in the many hours I spent learning from Ken, he shared his special project to gather his napkin scribbles into a book to share with the world. From cover to cover, Lean Leadership on a Napkin *takes the reader through a simple dialog with Ken, where he carefully plucks out the key components of Lean Leadership—what it means, why it matters, how to do it, and the impact of learning and applying the principles in whatever capacity you help people. Ken's deep knowledge of Toyota coupled with his passion and excellence in coaching and teaching provides the reader with an incredibly powerful approach for a Lean culture transformation.*

What specifically stands out in this book is his conversational nature, his transparency on common pitfalls, and his clear recommendations. Ken's mentorship is packaged beautifully in this book as an effective strategy to Lean Leadership and the subsequent organizational transformation, development, engagement, and the learning that follows.

— Stacey L. Graham, Executive Director, Client Executive Team,
The Resource Engineering & Hospitality Group,
Providence Health and Services

Ken and I met nearly a decade ago when I hired him to head up the Lean office in the Central Valley Region (CVR) of Sutter Health. I knew very little about Lean and Ken knew very little about healthcare operations. In retrospect, the strong personal and working relationship that we quickly developed supported our efforts to mutually learn and support one another in leading the Lean journey in the CVR. Ken's knowledge about Lean practices is extensive and is topped by his desire to help leaders discover and embrace its application in managing and leading an organization. He was very adept at using graphics and visuals to assist us in our learning process. We used those concepts a great deal in strategy development as well as with daily and monthly measurement tools.

Ken was uniformly supportive of all that were willing to be open about their concerns in the proper application of Lean-to-strategy and management processes. Ken took a risk by accepting the position as healthcare executives and managers can be quite resistant to changes offered by external sources, especially from those that have little—or no—direct healthcare experience. We also had some separate organizations within the region that were already committed to their Lean journey. My goal, and his task, was to develop a uniform approach of Lean across the region. We met resistance to this goal as it was seen as hindering the Lean efforts already in place in a subset of the region. Our geographic spread also contributed to challenges in attaining a uniform journey. Ultimately, his efforts were successful across the entire region.

His open communication style was a great match for me and the remainder of the leadership team and within 18 to 24 months we had made significant progress in the installation of Lean across our operating region of Sutter. Over time, because of his extensive Lean experience, Ken was utilized across the Sutter Health system and became a recognized expert as Lean developed in our company. I learned a great deal from Ken and that is something that many executives would not admit after 35+ years into a career in one industry. He helped increase my enjoyment for management and leadership in the last few years of my career. I am pleased that he has written this book and hopefully others will see that Lean principles can be applied to their own industry/company.

— David P. Benn, Former President,
Central Valley Region, Sutter Health

Lean Leadership on a Napkin

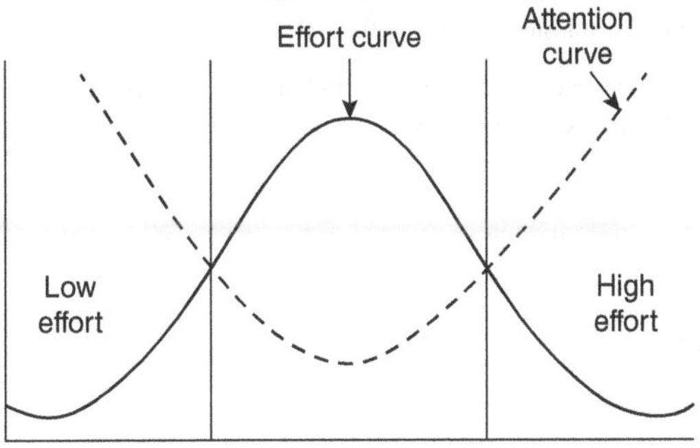

An Executive's Guide to Lean Transformation in Three Proven Steps

Ken Pilone

CRC Press
Taylor & Francis Group
Boca Raton London New York

CRC Press is an imprint of the
Taylor & Francis Group, an **informa** business
A PRODUCTIVITY PRESS BOOK

First published 2022
by Routledge
600 Broken Sound Parkway #300, Boca Raton FL, 33487
and by Routledge

2 Park Square, Milton Park, Abingdon, Oxon, OX14 4RN

Routledge is an imprint of the Taylor & Francis Group, an informa business

ISBN: 9781032066868 (hbk)
ISBN: 9781032066851 (pbk)
ISBN: 9781003203384 (ebk)

Typeset in ITC Garamond
by KnowledgeWorks Global Ltd.

Dedication

This book is humbly dedicated to my many mentors and coaches. You have inspired me and supported me in innumerable ways along my own lean journey and my own personal leadership transformation.

This is also dedicated to the next generation of lean leaders and lean coaches. It is my hope that what I have shared here will help in some small way to start you off on a higher plane than I did.

Likewise, I am so grateful for those who came before me. They gave me a head start from their own learning and wisdom that was so enthusiastically shared.

A special dedication to those of you whom I have had the honor and privilege of mentoring. I have learned so very much from you, especially your questions and insights. You have strengthened and humbled me.

Mostly, I have learned from those of you who have challenged and tested me. Your challenges have caused me to reflect deeply and to examine my own thinking more deeply. It is to you that I owe a debt of gratitude.

Finally, a word of thanks to those of you who came to me to learn about lean leadership and ended up teaching me as you took this work to the next level. I am so proud of you all! I pray that I have also made you proud. This is my only real measure of success. This will be my legacy.

Blessings to you all.

Contents

Foreword

Ken and I met over a decade ago; we were helping each of Sutter Health's five regions accelerate their lean journeys. Some were just starting some were fairly advanced. Ken's region was pretty advanced because they had Ken and his team. Over the years, they had consultants for their hospitals and group practices, but it was Ken's team that implemented the infrastructure to support a more evolved management system – that of Toyota.

When I first met Ken, I had no idea of the depth of his knowledge and experience. He was welcoming to our team, not a frequent response from internal lean groups when we were retained. His interest was leveraging and capitalizing on what we had to bring to the table; he was most interested in our ability to gain the curiosity and engagement of the executive team in deeply learning about Toyota and Lean; something that he had not seen occur within Sutter.

Ken had set up an entire system to support the learning of a new way to engage the front-line workers and a new way for leaders to appear at the front lines – as teachers and coaches as opposed to "solution" givers. He and his team had deployed extensive improvement capability, daily visual management, daily engagement of staff, leadership development and the daily tracking of aligned metrics – all connected to an annual strategy.

As we got to know each other, it was then that I learned of his deep experience and training outside of healthcare and specifically his career at Toyota. I always felt that Americans trained by and working in Toyota were potentially the very best teachers for US leaders. The fact that Ken and his team were retained by Toyota to develop their curriculum for lean leadership speaks volumes for the esteem in which they held him.

But probably that which most attracted me to Ken was his humility. His soft-spoken, patient, honest, friendly and humorous demeanor was always disarming and created the opportunity to learn. His commitment to respect for people and his own commitment to continuously learning and becoming better only modeled for those who met him that which could be.

It was not surprising then when we were having lunch one day, the subject of teaching and writing came up. He always believed in simple stories with which to teach. I remembered so many times in my life when the only handy piece of paper at a breakfast or lunch was a paper napkin … upon which many of my favorite notes were kept.

It seemed only natural that this humble and incredibly knowledgeable and experienced leader and teacher would write a book with the simplicity of "napkin scribbles" to tell a compelling and remarkably complete story of Toyota, Lean and how a leader can transform their organization in a way that no other management system has ever done.

Ken's book, really part one of a trilogy, if you will, focuses on a colorful and wonderfully readable introduction to Lean – its roots, its history, its principles, its misinterpretations and its deep appeal to those leaders who respect their customers and their workers. Using his very conversational writing style, punctuated with stories and simple but very complex analyses and methods, the reader is "pulled" through this story.

Whether you have never studied Lean or Toyota or whether you are at various stages of your Lean journey, you will find this book wonderfully informative and inviting. For those new to Lean and Toyota, you will find this to be an updated and far more efficient overview than any of the traditional texts used to introduce and teach this subject. For those more experienced, you will find this to be a wonderful refresher and reminder of why you were first attracted to Lean. And, for those of you who wish to reignite your Lean journey, you will find Ken an excellent guide.

Finally, I want to thank my dear friend Ken (with Tami side-by-side) for taking the time to write this book. All leaders in all industries will find it of great value.

Mike Rona
President, Rona Consulting Group

Preface

Prepare to be challenged. You may well find the contents here causing you to question the way you have led your whole professional career, the way that has gotten you to where you are today. You may wince at the changes that I will propose as contrary to all that you have been taught as the 'right way' to lead. Keep an open mind as we explore together this unique brand of leading called 'lean leadership'.

In case you're wondering, yes, there are a lot of lean leadership books already out there, but there's nothing quite like this! I have come to embrace this common wisdom, "If you can't explain something to a third grader, you probably don't understand it yourself!" The content here came from my own personal experience and my reflection on that experience and learning and extrapolations that will not be found anywhere else.

In sum, I built this to be a simple, easy-to-read resource guide for you, the senior organizational leader. I designed it to help you quickly look up lean and leadership reference material to use in your unique leadership role and organizational circumstances. Therefore, the primary focus here is not just germane to lean technology per se but to the surrounding culture that envelopes it as well.

It is also very much dedicated to a deep exploration, and perhaps reexamination, of your role as a leader. Lean, like any other cultural transformation, cannot be divorced from your leadership influence across the board. Your leadership style is completely intertwined with the culture you have created or fostered. Change your leadership style; change your culture. Change your culture; change your leadership style. They are two sides of the same coin.

Further, this guide is intended for leaders who are trying to figure out what the lean movement is all about and what, if anything, you as a leader should do about it. By the time you digest this book, you will have enough information to help you decide if you want to proceed further. If not, at least you will be making an informed and intelligent decision based on facts, not fads, and real-life, hands-on experience vs. traditional book learning.

Phase 1 is intended for leaders who have not yet made up their minds if they want to jump into the lean leadership pool headfirst. It's intended for those of you who have learned, probably the hard way, to be skeptical given all the management and business fads out there that have come and gone. As you have no doubt learned, most management fads, by their very nature, fade faster than bell bottoms! Interestingly, most have gone to great lengths to disavow the faddish nature of their approach. Each one professes to be the real deal. This is your first clue to run for cover.

Before we dive in more deeply, let me state clearly that my intent is to practice a fundamental and inherent lean philosophy, *keep it simple.* If anything about this book (or lean leadership itself for that matter) is hard to understand or unnecessarily complex, I have failed. This is a frequently violated principle of many lean resources out there! I passionately believe in the axiom *less is more.*

Finally, as this book is intended for you, the senior leader or executive, it is presented in that fashion. You will be exposed to the key points in an executive briefing style (i.e., bullets vs. paragraphs; sketches vs. text) when appropriate to the content.

Enjoy!

Acknowledgments

There are many people I would like to thank for help on this project. None is more important to acknowledge than my beautiful bride and joy, Tami. She worked tirelessly helping me at virtually every step of the way, from editing, to proofreading, to image creation, to tech support and design. Everything!

She provided the encouragement when I got the inevitable writer's block. She provided the push when it seemed I would never finish this ten-year labor of love. I simply could not have done it without her!

I would also like to thank my many mentors, friends and colleagues who encouraged me to do this. The actual idea for this book was an executive who I discovered had actually pinned many of my simple sketches on his wall. When I commented on it, he said, "You should staple all of these drawings together and call it a book!" And so it began.

A very special shout out goes to Mr. Mike Rona, President and Founder of the Rona Consulting Group, who saw the potential in me and believed that my work was worth sharing. With his ongoing, unwavering support, he breathed life into this work. I will be forever grateful, Mike.

Thank you all from the bottom of my heart!

Chapter 1

In the Beginning

Some Background

I retired after a nearly 20-year career at Toyota's US headquarters in Torrance, California. Let me state clearly at the outset, I refer to my time there as a 20-year internship. Working at Toyota was not easy. But for me it was an intense but richly rewarding experience which profoundly changed me and my perspective on leadership.

After leaving Toyota, I spent the remainder of my career teaching lean and translating it into other industries and business realms as both a private consultant and full-time employee serving in internal, lean-leadership consultant roles.

Who cares about Toyota? Most writers, speakers and other experts would quickly acknowledge that Toyota is the Mecca for lean practitioners. Almost every book out there says so. Toyota, I discovered, is a very different kind of place. Since I worked in Aerospace and other companies, public and private, prior to my immersion at Toyota, I had an up close and personal comparison of *normal* or traditional companies to Toyota.

To say that it was a culture shock is an understatement of epic proportions. Toyota seemed like such a weird place at first. Nothing seemed familiar. But slowly I learned and began to appreciate the culture and learned their language along the way. As I taught it to others, I eventually came to understand it myself even more deeply. Personally, I never want to work in a 'traditional' job or a 'normal' company again. Soon you will appreciate why.

One of the key roles I undertook with my colleagues while at the University of Toyota was the design, creation and deployment of a lean curricula that could be used anywhere, not just in manufacturing or production. We were commissioned by our parent company in Japan to do just that.

We designed a systematic process to assist any organization in any industry, beyond the factory floor, to maximize the potential benefits of a lean culture. Together we crafted a three-part approach to launch lean into new Toyota companies and divisions and for its suppliers and partners as well as other organizations far and wide. We also coined new terms and new methodologies that industry has now widely embraced.

To simplify our approach, we went back to basics. We divided the lean transformation process into three high-level strategic steps or 'phases': *Introduction*, *Integration* and *Internalization*. We framed it as the *I-3 approach*. The first, and by far the most important, part of this book is aimed at the *Introduction* phase, which we will dive into deeply.

Since we will be exploring this topic from a strategic vantage point, most of the nitty gritty, tactical work won't be covered in much detail here. This book is aimed primarily at top executives, and therefore the information is presented in executive summary form. The necessary details and specific action plans will come together with your team, probably with strong elbow-coaching support later. For now, stay focused on the long-term vision and strategy and avoid getting mired in the details.

This first part will help you figure out what lean is all about, how it might benefit you and your organization and how to avoid the major pitfalls many have fallen into. A word of caution, there is a lot of misinformation out there about lean and lean leadership. There are also highly exaggerated claims about its benefits, too. I encourage you to study these claims for yourself. As you explore other resources, check the credentials of their authors and consulting firms carefully! I will guide you on the best way to choose your partner(s) in this journey.

As the title implies, over many years of doing this, I have developed what I call my "Napkin Series" of lean leader education and executive coaching. Quite literally, these are the simple ways I use to help people, especially top leaders, understand lean by drawing simple sketches on napkins, paper towels, business cards, corners of tablecloths and the like. These drawings are not highly polished works of art. They have been created in very spontaneous ways.

I have drawn these crude sketches on picnic tables, car roofs and pickup truck hoods. It has evolved from countless lunch, dinner and happy hour coaching sessions when the only tools available were a napkin and a pencil. For the record, pencils are good; crayons are better.

In addition to explaining the core foundational elements of lean, I will also offer you some quick and easy ways to help you explain it to others. By the way, none of my sketches are copyrighted and all are intentionally easy to replicate. That is the point. You should be able to easily redraw them yourself to help you coach your own team through the process. Some of my sketches or similar versions have been inspired by or been passed on to me by my own mentors, but they aren't captured or catalogued anywhere else to my knowledge.

Two future parts in this series will cover *Integration* and *Internalization* in somewhat less depth but here we will give you a peak over the horizon to see what's coming if you decide to take the leap. However, when appropriate, you will see references made to the other phases throughout.

Note: Beware of slick PowerPoint presentations that offer to "introduce you to lean". They have their place but when the lights go down during a presentation, many people unconsciously slip into silent resistance mode. Some people are completely turned off by this 'sales job' approach.

While not necessarily a showstopper, most of my clients' decisions to dive into lean are traceable back more to our casual and frequent one-on-one discussions than they are from any formal presentations. Yes, there is a place for formal presentations, perhaps to the board of directors or large employee gatherings, but person-to-person dialogue is usually the best option in dealing with top executives and other key stakeholders, especially early on. See also "Nemawashi" in Chapter 4, "Lean Speak".

Let's keep it real; this is a big undertaking. It is not to be feared but to be approached as you would anything that has major culture change initiatives attached to it. Don't rush into it and don't expect to make a quick decision as to whether to adopt lean as your organization-wide operating system or cultural transformation process. And don't just jump into a new leadership style without a plan unless you want to freak out everybody with the 'new you'.

Take your time and do your homework. Research, study and collaborate with your executive team, other peers *and* your lean consultant(s) before you make a go/no-go decision. Keep in mind that within the locus of lean consultants, there are specialists of every description (i.e., manufacturing, supply chain, service industries, banking, finance, law enforcement, etc.). Your primary "lead" consultant will be like your primary physician who has multiple specialists at his/her disposal and can call on them or refer them to you as needed.

It goes without saying that I *STRONGLY* recommend partnering with a *seasoned* external coach! Don't go it alone! You wouldn't try to fly an airplane without an instructor first, would you? The investment you make in the early days of this journey will pay dividends quickly and can help you avoid costly mistakes down the road.

A Word about Cultural Transitions

I worked for many years and indeed had a ten-year second career in the healthcare industry. When we talk about cultural transitions, keep in mind that we are describing manifestly different ways of working.

One clear healthcare example of this is the Herculean transition from converting huge stacks of paper medical records to electronic medical data (EMR) data storage. Of course, the latter had enormous potential benefits, but the task to switch from old to new inspired all new dedicated industries just to help to bridge the transformation process. That conversion was daunting to say the least! Not an easy decision to be sure.

You should approach this transition with the same rigorous research, planning, realism and thoughtfulness that would be appropriate for any such large-scale effort. In the words of Ben Franklin, "Make haste slowly". Converting from a traditionally managed culture to a lean culture should be undertaken with clear-eyed realism of what is really involved and a very clear understanding of how it may affect you, your company and your leadership staff specifically.

It is worth noting that some think that they can just dabble in lean or just try out a few lean tools here and there. A simple Google search on lean tools will absolutely inundate you with possibilities. Sure, those that choose this approach are likely to pick up some short-term gains, but 'tool junkies' won't achieve the real potential of lean this way. Applying tools without the cultural underpinnings will result in disappointment, failure and cynicism.

The real problem here is that people tend to THINK they have 'adopted lean' by mimicking readily available lean tools. This is an illusion. Imagine trying to grow corn on the freeway. It doesn't matter how good the seeds are, they can't thrive in that condition. Just "planting" tools in the wrong organizational environment will likely have the same end result.

Some who have tried this approach have also fallen into the *illusion* of progress with lots of the trappings of lean and busy people conspicuously driving improvement events, having seminars, etc., but you will never achieve the full benefits of lean this way! It is like the saying that, if you vote, you therefore have a democracy! They vote in Iran, Venezuela and China, right? Copying behaviors without the culture to sustain them will fail. Once again, your primary coach will help you avoid this common trap.

So, putting up lean posters all over the place, developing slogans, having meetings, rallies, marketing projects and the like will only give you the appearance of a lean culture! This pseudo lean approach is like the difference between cheap chrome plate and sterling silver. It looks shiny at first, but the luster will eventually fade and peel away. Worse, in tough times, when resources are scarce, this is often the first place executives will look to cut costs.

By comparison, true lean organizations will invest more heavily in tough times because they realize the potential to survive may actually depend on the lean culture they have created. Think of it as a kind of organizational insurance. Even in tough times, you wouldn't cancel your fire insurance policy, would you?

But here is the good news: There ARE methods that will allow you to experiment, compartmentalize and learn quickly without committing to or driving an organization-wide transformation. It can be chunked up to make it far easier to implement. You may even isolate a specific department or unit with end-to-end process responsibility as a good place to start.

An example might be in HR in the recruiting process. Theoretically, they have complete responsibility to improve their work streams without very much spill over into other areas. These are great places to start. This will also help you to minimize the sticker shock when approaching the board of directors (BOD) and your chief financial officer (CFO).

This smaller scale "test of change" can be highly effective, especially if the process is articulated as part of a long-term, crawl-before-you-walk strategy. Check out the section on "model cells". For what it's worth, my favorite word in the lean vocabulary is "experiment". Soon you will appreciate why. More on this later.

One final note: As stated earlier, none of what I am offering here is copyrighted even though it is primarily my own original work. I am at a point in my life where I just want to leave a positive legacy and "leave it all on the field" so to speak. Nothing more.

I simply want you to learn and to use this methodology. Why? I think you will see that once lean leadership is properly understood, demystified and deployed, it can and will dramatically improve and strengthen your organization and change lives (especially yours) for the better. It did mine.

Chapter 2

The Introduction Phase

OK, let's dive into this thing a little deeper. Figure 2.1 is an example of one napkin drawing and the 'dialogue' that would accompany it. Let's set the stage. The typical setting is with me as the lead consultant/coach sitting across a cafeteria table or on a tailgate at a construction site in an informal meeting with an organizational leader, or maybe two or three tops. More than that becomes unwieldy crowd control and stifles rich discussion and relationship building.

Typical Dialogue

Here is the first 'napkin' drawing …

From Figure 2.1, you can appreciate that most of the heavy lifting, let's call it *Level of Effort*, occurs in the *Introduction* phase. That is, when you will experience the most resistance and where you will need the highest level of persistence, patience, and, yes, *push* necessary to reach the pinnacle.

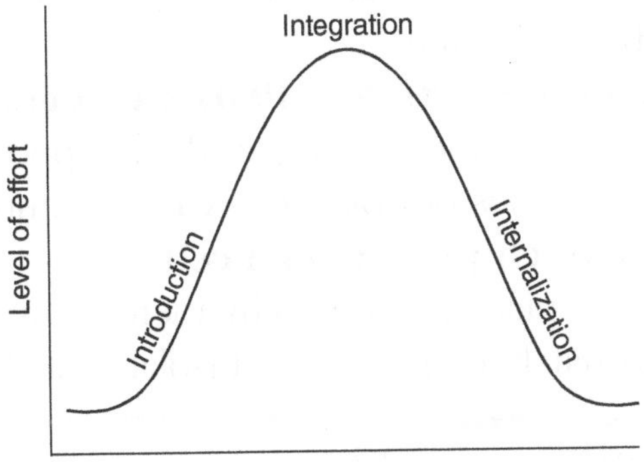

Figure 2.1

Note: You will hear the expression of pull vs. push used in a different context later. Here, I am referring to the effort that necessary to overcome negative inertia.

These are some typical activities in the *Introduction* phase:

- **Selection of a coach/consultant team**
  - Perhaps the most important decision of all!
  - Success or failure depends on this; roles are defined here
- **Mapping out of the plan and timeline**
  - How long will the transformation take?
  - Building a high-level three- to five-year implementation Gantt chart
- **Identifying Key Performance Indicators (KPIs): Who are your customers and what do they want from you?**
  - Positioning lean as a means to an end; not the end in itself
  - Staying grounded in the business: KPIs are the 'what'; lean is the 'how'
  - The customer is the 'who'
- **Creating the burning platform/sense of urgency**
  - No burning platform? Start a fire!
  - Ask yourselves, 'What will get folks excited about this?'
- **Establishing a preliminary budget**
  - This is a *rolling wave* type project; budget must evolve over time
  - Align with the CFO and BOD
- **Evaluating the people landscape**
  - Who's available to help? Early adopters? Local champions?
  - Where is resistance most likely to surface? Develop a plan to overcome it
- **Aligning with critical support departments and unions**
  - What are the key functions and groups you will need to bring aboard?
  - Align with HR! Corporate?
- **One-on-one meetings with key BOD members**
  - Plan on how to brief them and gain their support
  - What concerns, issues or objections can you anticipate?
- **Deciding on a launch plan; model cell**
  - Where's the best place to start? Why there? Why now?
  - Can it be adequately contained and isolated without undue spillover?
- **Training**
  - Explain 'what's happening'? for top leadership, supervision, all hands
  - Specific, targeted training plan development: who gets what?

- **5S (see Chapter 4, "Lean Speak", for a description)**
  - Fast-start process; creates a buzz; positive and energizing experience
  - Quick gains; obvious and tangible results. Builds momentum
- **Communication planning**
  - Develop a communication matrix
  - Tailored messaging for all groups
- **Industry/enterprise specific plans**
  - What is unique? What can be learned from others?
  - Adopt or adapt? Leveraging local networks

Here are some of the questions your employees will ask that must be answered during the *Introduction* phase:

- *What is lean?*
- *Why do we care?*
- *How does it benefit the organization?*
- *How will this change things around here?*
- *What will be different?*
- *Why here?*
- *Why now?*
- *What's in it for me?*
- *How much effort is required?*
- *How do I learn more about it?*
- And the biggie: *Will I lose my job?*

As you can also imagine, failure at the *Introduction* phase will result in the transformation process falling back on itself! Here's a sobering thought: it is extremely hard to recover from this! Failure in the *Introduction* phase is the single most frequent reason why lean transformations die an early death.

Often you will hear something like, "*We tried it, but it didn't work for us*". Chances are 90% that the failure occurred during, or is traceable back, to the *Introduction* phase! Together with your consulting team, you will map out a plan to *prevent* the failure to launch a trap as well as to institute measures to prevent backsliding.

Note: Phase one requires DEEP conversation and even deeper thinking. Go slow here. It is sometimes better to just walk away at this point rather than begin in a half-hearted way. Should failure occur here, widespread cynicism will likely be the result. This will make your next restart attempt ten times harder! As we say in lean circles, "*Sometimes you have to go slow to go fast*".

If you sense that you are presently in a cultural 'steady state', chances are you will not be feeling much back pressure, at least until you start to change things. Resistance to change will be minimal or non-existent if nothing is changing, right?

Remember from high school physics class, "Bodies at rest tend to stay at rest"? We learned then that additional horsepower is required to overcome negative inertia. This is equally true when it comes to cultural changes. Cultural negative inertia is a very predictable phenomenon, but we have also learned that it can be overcome. Nevertheless, many leaders are surprised at the amount of resistance they encounter, often from unexpected sources.

Keep in mind that most of the resistance you will encounter will be converted. Rarely will your team openly resist. Some might do so among themselves in the break room or other spaces but often will not risk the potential consequences of public opposition. Cynicism is a real threat to your success. Don't deny it or gloss over it. Take it seriously and tackle it head on!

Be especially alert to body language and nuance, too. A simple eye roll can communicate volumes. Especially if it comes from a known opinion leader in your organization. Remember that sometimes resistance is institutionalized in the form of unions, for example. We will dive more deeply into this unique challenge later. Suffice it for now that it can be overcome. I've seen many people who started out as the most unlikely to support this transformation become your most trusted allies and champions. This is not uncommon.

You will probably have to use your own intuition and people skills to try to understand where their heads are, both individually and collectively. Remember that resistance to change is natural and, like gravity, must be overcome to achieve lift. TIP: Stay alert to phrases like, *"Let me play devil's advocate"*. This is code for, *"I ain't buyin' what you're selling"*. Your coach will work with you to identify pockets of resistance beforehand, but perhaps more importantly, identify areas of opportunity! Divide and conquer is a useful notion. Once again, see Nemawashi in Chapter 4, "Lean Speak".

The status quo is a formidable force; some might even say it is the enemy, which will require uncommon will and vision to overcome. From my former clients who have reflected on this stage, they are consistent in their assessment that no matter how much they expected the status quo to slow them down, it was far worse than they expected! To a person. So, like my dad used to say, *"Expect the worst and you won't be disappointed"*. Maybe that's overstated, but you get the idea.

Think about this. It may surprise you that people resist change even if the change is obviously better than the current state. I suppose, it is just the way we are wired. For example, people stay in jobs far longer than they expected because, while they really hate the job, they fear the trauma of change even more. The result is that they have an unhappy work life and then become bitter and negative.

So, expect resistance. Acknowledge it; honor it and plan for it. But again, do NOT fear it! Along with your lean coach, I will help you to develop a strategy to minimize the gravitational pull of resistance and help you to counteract it with just the right amount of force to overcome it.

Remember, lean has been implemented *successfully* literally thousands of times. In hindsight through comprehensive and rigorous autopsies, we have learned many valuable lessons from those who have failed, helping us guide you to avoid making the same often irreversible mistakes they made. You can do it.

End of Dialogue #1

OK, so let's also acknowledge the obvious. Yes, of course, there have been and always will be setbacks and even complete failures. Even extraordinarily successful implementations are rarely linear or sequential. Sometimes it's even a *two steps forward* and *one step back* scenarios. If properly set up, you will have built in backstops to prevent going all the way back to square one.

I like to imagine a lean culture transformation as akin to driving up a long, steep mountain road. To get to the summit, you first must navigate around tight turns and switchbacks while staying on the alert for falling rocks and sheer cliffs. You may even encounter patches of fog or icy spots here and there. Some stretches are steep inclines followed by deep drops. You may wonder, *"Why are we going down here? Shouldn't we be climbing?"* Our compass swings wildly, but we expect that as we make our way to the top.

We have to switch continuously between the gas and the brakes, and steer continuously and forcefully. We may even look down on the road when we just traveled that is now far below us. One thing we can't do is let up or we'll roll backwards into oblivion. But we might choose to take advantage of turnouts and scenic overlooks along the way to acknowledge and celebrate our progress. Eventually, we know that the view from the summit is worth it! To me, this is a very fitting metaphor of the lean journey.

Looking again at our drawing (Figure 2.1) and beyond the initial *Introduction* phase, as resistance is gradually overcome, we expect to see the required level of effort (LOE), especially from the executive team, lessening. Slowly but surely, you will build partnerships from within that will ease your own personal burden considerably. As you progress up this hill, you will pick up support from early adopters who will share the load. I have learned that a measure of evangelism comes in handy here.

Story Time: *Show Me Your Weed, Man!*

I remember vividly an experience that I had in college. Reluctantly, I had registered for a class in Botany. I had to sign up for a science class and it was the only available option. I remember one specific class; we were all assembled, waiting for our professor. We watched the clock hoping that we could leave after the required 10 minutes if he didn't show up.

Just as we were about to leave, so he ran into the room, sweating profusely. He was disheveled and looked like he had slept in his clothes. Out of breath, he yelled as he entered the class, "*Sorry I'm late everybody. Come to the front of the room right away!*" "*Come, come up now!*" he said. We giggled among ourselves and grudgingly made our way to a table at the front of the room. "*Everybody gather 'round the table'*", he told us as he gradually caught his breath.

At this point he pulled out a weed from his briefcase and ever so gently laid it out on the table. He cradled it as if it were the Shroud of Turin. "*Look*", he said. "*Look what I have discovered!*" The joy in his voice was unmistakable. We looked at each other and thought, this guy has really lost it!

"*I was stuck in traffic on the 405 on my way here*", he said. "*I was stopped dead. I happened at that moment to look out my window and saw this plant growing up through the asphalt along the median. I jumped from my car to get a closer look. I had to find a way to bring it here. I had to use my car keys to dig it up*", he shared. We just looked at each other trying to keep from laughing out loud.

"*Do you know what this is?*" he asked of no one in particular. "*A weed?*" somebody said, and we all lost it at that point. When the laughter died down, we could see he was not amused. He dropped a big reference book on the table in front of us called *The Flora of California* (or something like that). Up to that point, the class had used that book to learn how to classify different types of plants. "*Look it up!*" he said indignantly.

We opened the book and used the analytic process, he had taught us to try to identify his weed. We were not able to find it. After we gave up, he said, *"Do you know why you can't find it?"* We shook our heads numbly. He said, *"Because it isn't there! It isn't there because it isn't supposed to be in California"*, he said, his eyes widening. *"This just isn't supposed to be here!"* he repeated.

Now we were curious. We set out to dig deeper into our books to see if we could find it somewhere else. Sure enough, it was not indigenous to California but was common in the Southern states. *"How did it get here?"* we asked. He just shrugged. *"Class"*, he said more calmly, *"this is a discovery! I'm sure of it"*. *"I can't wait to write it up for the journals. Maybe they will even name it after me!"* he beamed.

We were hooked! At that moment, we saw what passion could do. He inspired us with the story of his weed, and we ended up high-fiving him and each other. Somehow, we all felt part of his triumph and shared that moment with him. From that moment on, our class felt a unique bond with each other, our professor and his weed.

Sadly, I don't remember his name, but I do remember how he made me feel! I went from being bored and distracted to being completely engaged in a topic that I had zero interest in before that day. He ignited something dormant within in me. He helped me realize later that passion is contagious. Great leaders know this.

This happened to me a long time ago. And yet it has stuck with me all these years as one of those 'moments' in life you just can't forget. It is also an example of the power of passion and the power to ignite others with it. Just think about how much more compelling your story will be as you evangelize lean. Your passion, your spark, will inspire others who will gather around your table wanting to see what you see in it. Think about it.

And, While You Are at It, Think about This

If you ever learned a new skill, you would probably remember how it felt. For me it was learning to ski. There was a point where I was certain that I could never do it! It was the most unnatural thing to me, and I thought I must have looked ridiculous attempting it. I was embarrassed and was tempted to quit many, many times! Now I ski effortlessly, thoughtlessly. I don't even remember what it was like NOT to know how to ski.

Do you have any experiences like that? When you think back on all the new things you have learned and the new skills you have acquired in your personal and professional life, you will quickly realize that you already have what it takes to accomplish this, too.

So, in addition to explaining the core elements of lean transformation and how to do it, I hope to also ignite a passion in you. I will offer you some quick and easy ways to help you explain it to others, too. That is the point of my crude little drawings.

As you have seen in the earlier example, these are the simple ways I use to help people, especially leaders, to understand lean by using metaphors, drawings on napkins, paper towels, business cards, corners of tablecloths and the like. Images tend to stick in peoples' minds far longer than words. You will remember a picture even after the words, or who spoke them, have vaporized.

Chapter 3

What Do I Need to Know about Lean Leadership?

After over 35 years of doing this, I have concluded that basic concepts and tools of lean can be reduced to just three words: ***applied common sense***! No more. Anything anybody says to the contrary has missed the point. As with so many other disciplines, others have made a living trying to make it more complicated than it is.

Humble Beginnings

Toyota's earliest beginnings came from its rural, agricultural roots. The very name of the founding family *Toyoda* (yes, with a "D") means "green field". The founders in the beginning were what we in the United States might call *country bumpkins.*

They were simple farmers who grew up in an environment of resource scarcity, but who also possessed an abundance of common sense and resourcefulness. It is from those early lessons that Toyota has emerged as the company we know today. And, 'lean', which is a term applied by others to describe what they observed at Toyota, is similarly based on some very basic foundational principles that we will explore in depth later.

So, don't let anybody tell you that lean is complicated. It is simple, but it's not easy. The great philosopher and humorist Will Rogers famously said about opinionated people, "It isn't what we don't know that gives us trouble, it's what we know that ain't so".

So, my message to you is don't let folks convince you to hire them as consultants if they have over-complicated it and made it seem like you need somebody smart to understand lean. On the other hand, do call on seasoned professionals who make their living *simplifying* your enterprise and have a track record of successful lean implementations.

In Chapter 13, "Some Great Resources", I will show you what to look for and how to figure out, the best way to select solid consultant support.

Back to History ...

Here are some of the key players you should know about. The original founder of the company was a guy named Sakichi Toyoda. He grew up in a hilly area of rural Japan in what you would imagine to be a log cabin surrounded by a simply wonderful bamboo forest. You can hear the trees clacking together in the wind. What an awesome treat for the senses! It left an indelible impression on me.

In the main area of their simple home was an open space with a hibachi of sorts used primarily for warmth and cooking. In a corner, a very crude wooden loom sat idle. Not much else to see. It did help me understand the truly humble beginnings of this incredible company, however.

In the late 1800s and early 1900s, the Toyoda family was struggling to make ends meet. Japan's economy at the time was a simple system of bartering and horse-trading like in so many other underdeveloped countries.

Sakichi's dad was a farmer who supplemented the family income by selling fabric his wife made at home on a crude, wooden, and handmade loom. While he was growing up, Sakichi, as well as other Japanese people, became aware that Japan had fallen far behind the rest of the developed world. They were shocked and embarrassed by the advancements made outside their country during their self-imposed isolation.

When Commodore Perry from the US Navy and his frightening steamships arrived in Japanese waters, the Japanese saw how advanced the 'outside world' had become, and there was a collective gasp across their country as they realized how seriously behind the rest of the world they had become.

They were behind in nearly every respect thanks to their prior isolationist mentality. A real sense of urgency and panic spread across the country.

The emperor reached out to the entire country with a single but inspiring message, paraphrased as "We need to catch up. And fast!" He asked that every citizen start to think of ways to do so. He wanted to encourage young Japanese to start using their innate gifts and talents of invention and innovation to start to close those huge gaps.

Heeding the emperor's call, Sakichi looked around at his humble surroundings to find what, if anything, he could do to help his country. But what could a simple, rural farm boy do? All he saw was his father farming and his mother slaving away on her crude old handmade loom. "That's it!" he realized. He decided that he could indeed make a better loom to help her, other weavers, and who knows, maybe the country.

From my research of his early life, it seems that Sakichi was an odd child, not one who mixed easily with other kids in his age. Some body say he had a similar personality to young Thomas Edison. Apparently, he had trouble getting along with boys in his own age, who teased him about engaging in weaving, which was, after all, considered as women's work at the time.

Nevertheless, he was able to resist the relentless peer pressure and soldiered on in his work, deriving motivation from within, hoping that he might well be doing something important for his beloved Japan.

And so, he focused his energies entirely on this pursuit, even drawing design ideas and sketches by candlelight. As time went by, not only did he succeed in making many improvements to his looms, but he also became known as the inventor of the finest looms in the entire world, even better than the best Europe had to offer. This is still true today.

Indeed, Sakichi is acknowledged today as one of the single most significant figures in Japanese history. In Japan, he is still revered as no less an icon than the legendary Thomas Edison in the United States! In fact, he is widely considered the "King of Japanese Inventors", with over 100 patents to his name.

One of his earliest inventions—as he pursued powered, automatic looms—was a startlingly simple innovation. He realized that even a single broken strand of yarn, if not detected in the weaving process, caused defective fabric that had to be either completely scrapped or which required precious time to repair even if it was detected soon after it occurred. Later, we will dive deeply into the notion of the waste resulting from this kind of rework.

But how could he prevent the defects, he wondered? He had an idea! His simple but breakthrough idea was to apply tension to each strand of yarn with a simple weight so that, if any of the threads broke, the weight would drop and engage a device to automatically stop the machine, thus *preventing* defective yarn from entering the loom in the first place.

Not only did this technology stop defects at their source, but it also allowed a single operator to monitor many looms simultaneously, knowing that they would simply stop if a thread broke and lay idle until the problem was corrected. He figured that having a machine lay idle was less of a problem than that created by producing a defective product and the required time-consuming rework. As a result, he managed to accomplish not only higher quality and efficiency but also a huge reduction in rework as well.

These devices are referred to generally as *poka yoke* devices. They are essentially physical mechanisms for error proofing and thus allow the building in of quality at the source. It made defective cloth essentially impossible to produce! What a concept!!!

Note: Nowadays, there are many modern and even electronic iterations of the same basic concept. By the way, you will find a related Japanese term of *Jidoka*, (built in quality) in Chapter 4, "Lean Speak".

In time, Sakichi became an incredibly famous and wealthy man. He traveled the world to share his knowledge and in search of the latest ideas, opportunities and inspirations. One of those trips brought him by steamship to the United States, where he fell in love with the newfangled automobile. A flame was lit inside him!

Inspired like never before, Sakichi gave his young engineering college graduate son, Kiichiro, all the money he had saved up on one single condition that he must use it all to develop a car in Japan for the Japanese, a challenge that Kiichiro, somewhat apprehensively, accepted. And so, Toyota as we know it today was born.

So then, Kiichiro became the founder of the Toyoda *car* business. Suffice it that he had learned well from his father. He was smart, industrious and curious. Having grown up in his father's textile and loom businesses, he absorbed many of the founding principles that had made them so successful.

He adapted them from the very beginning to prove that Japan could build a car as good as any in the United States. In fact, their first car, a 1936 Toyoda Model AA Sedan, was a hybrid of sorts that used a Ford drivetrain and a Chrysler Airflow body, both considered the best of the day.

Little Known Fact: What's in a Name?

In those days at Toyota, a national contest was held to both name their new cars and to stimulate interest in it. The current name "Toyota" (with a "T") was the contest winner. Why? Because the name was easier to pronounce, it sounded like the founder's name and, when rendered in Japanese kanji, a form of Japanese writing, it used eight brush strokes, which evokes a notion of good luck and opportunity.

An interesting side note about Kiichiro. He was known to always be grimy. Even though he was the founder and the son of the legendary Sakichi, he loved to get his hands dirty, literally. As an engineer, he wanted to learn how things worked and how to fix things. Accordingly, he would always be covered in grease. This is not what executives do, right? When his team teased him about it, he would respond, "Why aren't you dirty, too?" This will become more relevant as we learn about the notion of going to the *Gemba* (the actual workplace).

Kiichiro and his early team started the process of producing a car by copying and reverse engineering other cars, primarily Fords, that were on the roads in Japan at the time. He adapted good ideas from wherever he could find them to fit the unique circumstances at hand.

Breakthrough: by reverse engineering, Kiichiro was able not just to produce a car but, more importantly, to develop the materials, processes, skills and tools necessary to do so. The importance of this approach cannot be overstated! As a result of reverse engineering, he was able to create an entire end-to-end manufacturing infrastructure as a foundation on which to build and adapt for years to come!

Not the least of the ideas Kiichiro adopted were those quality ideas brought from America's own J. Edwards Deming, after World War II. Deming brought critical quality theory to post-war Japan, which was devastated after the war. Kiichiro and his team listened intently, learned deeply and applied those lessons to make their products better and better. Who knows, maybe one day they could even begin to export, they imagined. Export indeed!

Story Time: *Getting Dirty*

As stated above, Kiichiro had learned the benefits of going to where the work was being performed and where problems surfaced. Here's a related example from my own learning.

I was visiting one of our manufacturing plants in Kentucky. At the time, Camrys were made there. I was touring the part of the plant where accessories were added to an otherwise completed vehicle.

While I was observing the process of a radio being installed into the dashboard, I overheard the lead person impatiently asking the technician, "What's taking so damn long?" I asked the lead person, "What was going on there?" He said that there was a new radio product that they were installing and that the technician had significantly exceeded his allotted time (Takt time) to complete the installation.

I asked the lead, "Why is he taking longer than you expect?" He shrugged and said, "He's just working too slowly". I followed up with the question, "How well do you understand this installation process and his problems with it?" He said, "I used to be in the same job before I was promoted to lead, so I know it very well!"

I asked if he would mind if I tried the installation myself? Amused he said, "Sure, why not?!" The next one is yours. Here's the standard work (SW) (think detailed instructions with timelines). I studied the SW document, removed my coat and tie and crawled under the dashboard, contorting my body into a weird, upside down, twisted and very unnatural way.

I held a flashlight in my teeth and attempted to make color-coded wiring connections that were hidden from view by feel! "What is the point of color coding if you can't even see the connection being made?" I muttered to myself.

Eventually I managed to confirm that the wires were indeed connected, hopefully correctly. As I managed to crawl backwards onto the shop floor, I realized that I had cut myself somewhere during the process and now I had to clean up the blood I left behind.

I was, by pure beginner's luck, able to make the correct connections on the first try. Had I not, I would have had to go back under and reverse them! Needless to say, I tripled the required takt time but gained a much deeper understanding of the real problems in the process. Not a pleasant experience.

When I reported my experience back to the lead person, I simply said, "I think I now understand the problem better than you do". He replied, "Point made".

Little Known Fact: Unscathed by WWII—Almost

Toyota had largely escaped the destruction of the war, as it was producing trucks and ambulances for the war effort and not on the list of priority targets for American bombers. Nevertheless, on the last day of the war in Japan, one of Toyota's factories was bombed and destroyed as an opportunistic secondary target.

Another key figure in the history of lean is a guy named Taiichi Ohno. He is generally regarded as the "Father of TPS", the legendary ***Toyota Production System***. He was formerly in the loom business working for Kiichiro's father, Sakichi, but came over as a Section Head in the fledgling and highly secret car production experiment. We call them "skunk works" here.

While many isolated improvements were being made constantly, Ohno is the first to combine them into a coherent system. He put all the puzzle pieces together, as it were. More than any other single person, he is generally thought of as the true originator of what is now called lean.

Little Known Fact: Mustache Man

An interesting side note about Ohno, he was called "mustache man" behind his back. It was uncommon to wear a mustache in those days. But he did so because he felt it made him seem more manly despite his small stature. He was largely ignored by his team of production workers, however, and was known to be a serious and habitually grouchy guy.

Despite his less-than-remarkable personality, Ohno was nevertheless able to make huge differences in the plant primarily by appealing directly to Kiichiro and to Kiichiro's uncle Eiji Toyoda, also a top executive, for their intervention on his behalf.

At that time, Toyota was still emulating Ford. This meant an obsession with individual performance, high volume production and piece work. As a result, large piles of completed but unused components would be "pushed" down the line and would pile up at the next operator's station. Here's how Ohno got that fixed … I love this story …

Since Ohno knew that his requests tended to be largely ignored, he shrewdly leveraged his relationship with Eiji to get the job done. Unlike Taiichi, Eiji was loved and respected by all. It turns out that Ohno was able to get one huge change made through invoking Eiji's authority and direction.

At Ohno's dogged and passionate request, Eiji put out a new rule that simply required that every production worker *carry home* (on their bicycles) any excess inventory that they had produced at the end of their shift (pity the engine block production workers).

As a result, producers only made what could be consumed by the next worker as needed. They were NOT to produce anything until it was pulled (requested) by the downstream customer. This meant that, yes, they were idle at times. Sound familiar?

Note: By being idle and by being *conspicuous* about it, Ohno could see where there were peaks and valleys in the workflow. He even drew circles on the factory floor (later called "Ohno circles") and insisted that idle workers stand in them to make it obvious where excess capacity existed and hence, line balancing and reapportioning worker's effort could occur more readily. Watching the process from those circles, they also had an opportunity to critically observe what was really happening over many cycles. These circles are still in use today all over the world.

This provided yet another piece in the lean puzzle to fall into place, level or even flow to relieve over-burden in some pockets of the line. See also, "Heijunka, Mura and Muri" in Chapter 4.

Also, to offset any salary penalties, they shifted from paying workers on a piecework basis to a team-based compensation model, where they all benefited from the overall efficiency of the plant and production volumes equally. This was yet another component of Ohno's clever plan to enhance communication and teamwork!

And so, with the stroke of a pen, *voila,* several problems were solved simultaneously. Just like that, no more excess inventory (also known as Work in Process (WIP)), improved teamwork, better communication and a more even or level distribution of effort. Importantly, this rule ultimately led to Ohno's dream of a true pull system where nothing is produced until it is required, or pulled, by the next worker (internal customer) downstream with effort being shared equally from one end of the production line to the other.

Pulling work vs. pushing work allowed the entire factory to move at the pace or pull of market demand, thus speeding up or slowing down as demand fluctuated was now achievable. See also, "Takt Time" in Chapter 4.

Shifting Market Demand

So, let's shift gears here and talk about demand.

We all know that America fell in love with Japanese products in the mid-70s. After the first oil embargo, we Americans were looking for alternative, fuel-efficient vehicle choices. As our obsession with huge gas-guzzling cars waned, we discovered high-quality and fuel-efficient Toyotas (as well as Datsuns [now Nissan] and, later, Hondas).

The oil embargo turned out to be a stroke of luck for Toyota! But, as we know, *luck is what happens when preparation meets opportunity.* In that nexus, if either value goes to zero, you have "no luck". They had an opportunity now.

They had to be prepared to seize the sudden demand overseas. This was the time. Ready or not, they had to dive in headfirst or be forever left behind! They had to muster the resources and, more importantly, the will to do so.

Meanwhile in the United States, as the Big 3 (GM, Ford and Chrysler) struggled to compete, their inefficient gas-guzzling products became obsolete virtually overnight. Albeit grudgingly, they started to grasp and accept TPS. One by one, they overcame their resistance to learn from Japan and sought to develop new relationships with their Japanese competitors. Ultimately, partnerships were formed, and everyone benefited. Toyota had a virtually untapped market while the Big Three had the opportunity to utterly transform and revitalize themselves.

Story Time: *The GM and Toyota Partnership*

GM, along with the other Big 3 US car companies, were struggling mightily during this transition. Their early efforts to shift to smaller, more fuel-efficient cars brought us the likes of the Chevy Citation and its cousin the Cadillac Cimarron, along with the much maligned Vega. These were epic flops among others like the Chrysler K cars (Valiant and Dart), the Ford's Pinto and Escort and the AMC Pacer. This was indeed the low ebb of quality for made-in-America vehicles.

Meanwhile, they pursued protective legislation, import tariffs, the infamous "chicken tax" and other available means to try to slow down the arrival of Japanese imports. They attempted to placate both their unions and the federal government by blaming the Japanese for dumping products in the United States at or below their production cost. And to the American populace, the Japanese car companies were portrayed as the enemy of American workers and the reason for the loss of American jobs.

Nevertheless, inexorably, Japanese products steadily grew their market share in the United States. Efforts to regulate them ultimately failed and forced US manufacturing to come to grips with the reality that consumers now wanted and began to expect cars that were high-quality, fuel-efficient AND reasonably priced. We wanted and had learned to expect all three attributes at the same time. Imagine that!

Enter NUMMI

Even after GM had slowly conceded that companies like Toyota did in fact produce cars that Americans wanted, they quickly reminded us that the Japanese 'quality' imports could ONLY be produced in Japan and ONLY with non-union Japanese workers who were paid pennies on the dollar. Ultimately, things came to a head in the mid-1980s.

It was then that Lee Iacocca, Senior Big 3 leaders whose head industry spokesman, Lee Iacocca, issued a collective challenge to Toyota et al. by saying essentially, *We concede that you are able to produce low-cost, high-quality products in Japan, but let's see you do it* HERE *in America! Let's see if you can build high-quality products on American soil with American* UNION *workers!*

Eiji Toyoda, then the Toyota chairman, accepted the challenge. Much to the chagrin of his own board of directors, who also questioned if building the same high-quality products in the United States with American union workers were indeed possible, Eiji pressed his case. He reasoned that it would prove once and for all that it was the *system* that produced the quality, not just the workers.

Properly trained, he believed that workers using TPS would carry the day ANYWHERE and with any kind of workers. Eventually, he was able to convince his board that this was a grand experiment and one that would permanently lay to rest the excuses made by GM and the other Big 3 companies. He argued that Toyota would never be in a better place than at that exact moment in history to prove that TPS, the system, trumps the workers every day of the week.

In the months to follow, Toyota would begin shopping for a suitable place to make landfall in the United States to try out its experiment. After a small experiment, 'aka 'test of change', in a sheet metal fabrication sub-assembly plant in Long Beach, California, called Atlas Fabricators, they were convinced TPS would indeed work in America and with union workers!

As it turns out, GM had a shuttered plant in Fremont, California. They had closed it due to poor quality and dreadful labor management relations; laying off the workers and closing the plant was the only remaining recourse. The Fremont plant had a dreadful reputation, having been dead last in product quality, absenteeism, worker safety and customer satisfaction. It was simply the worst plant among all GM's plants anywhere in the world.

Enter Toyota. A deal was struck with Toyota and GM in partnership to reopen the shuttered plant under its new name, New United Motor Manufacturing, Inc. (NUMMI). In its negotiations with GM, Toyota had been led to believe that it had reserved the right to hire its own workers, since the deal called for Toyota to run the plant using TPS. But, as GM buckled to the will of the united auto workers (UAW), a new condition was imposed.

GM agreed that, yes, Toyota would indeed run the plant and hire its employees BUT it must agree to hire most of them from those former UAW workers who had been previously laid off from that same plant by GM! These were the same workers who were told that losing their jobs was the fault of the Japanese! Anybody but Eiji would have folded up their briefcase and left on the spot. Toyota ultimately conceded and the deal was done. They started to produce vehicles in NUMMI using union workers that were the best in the world. Simply put, they went from worst to first in less than two years!

There's a *LOT* more to this story but these highlights should give you enough information to engage in a reasonably intelligent conversation about lean. In fact, much of the above, especially the historical and personal anecdotes, will be new to most people. Use them to impress your friends.

Chapter 4

Lean Speak—Do I Need to Learn Japanese?

As is the case with any business discipline like HR or IT, lean has its own unique vocabulary and jargon. I'll call it *lean speak*. Since most of this work had its origins in Toyota, it is not surprising that many of the terms used are Japanese. You have already been introduced to some common ones mentioned earlier.

Over the years, as I have helped my clients through their lean transformations, there is a constant, predictable, recurring question, "Do we have to learn Japanese? Really?" or its parallel question, "Can't we just speak English?" In the early days of my consulting practice, I would strenuously stress the need to learn the language of lean regardless of its roots.

But over the ensuing years, I have learned to just agree to try to use English whenever an equivalent term is available, but I have a confession. Nowadays I usually ignore their requests, knowing full well that they will end up unconsciously using Japanese anyway despite their protests. You will, too.

As is the case with learning any new language (or culture), immersion is best. I have discovered that, through repetition, my clients have assimilated the Japanese terms as easily as people have with other 'foreign' words like pizza or croissant. Our American brand of English is so riddled with vocabulary from other languages that we fail to even notice that they originated someplace else. Sushi anyone?

My advice to you as an executive is simply to be open to the fact that you are learning a new language *and* culture. You will be absorbing the terms used naturally and will end up with lean fluency without even consciously trying. Trust me on this.

To get you started, below is a description of some of the more common terms you will hear and will begin using. For an exhaustive list, see Some Great Resources, Chapter 13, for a list of reference books including *Lean Lexicon,* which contains an exhaustive dictionary of lean vocabulary. Keep in mind that a more complete understanding of many of these terms and their impact on your new lean culture follows in later chapters.

Common Lean Terminology

Here is a partial alphabetical list of some of the more common terms you will find here in the context of lean. The most significant and/or common terms are in *italics.* What is important here is the broader meaning or use of the terms.

- **2P**
  - *General definition*: People and Process Reevaluation.
  - *Broader meaning*: This is a methodology for improving flow within an existing plant, office, etc., where physical changes are either impossible or impractical (aka brown field).
- **3P**
  - *General definition*: Production, Preparation and Process Reevaluation.
  - *Broader meaning*: This is a methodology employed when designing a flow in a new plant, business, location, etc., from scratch (aka green field).
- ***5S***
  - *General definition*: A process used to clean up and sustain an efficient, safe, clutter-free work area.
  - *Broader meaning*: A process to make work more productive, safer and less stressful by eliminating non-essential items and making it easier to find needed tools, equipment and supplies. The goal here is to minimize excess inventory and always have the right amount or range of a commodity readily available. Think min-max or par levels.
- ***Five Why's Root Cause Analysis (RCA)***
  - *General definition*: A repeatable process to reveal the true cause of a gap or problem.

- *Broader meaning*: The process of rigorous RCA is to get below the surface of an unexpected situation or gap to discover its origins or root cause. This is done by asking the question "why" five times. The number five is not a rigid rule. It is intended to encourage people to continue to dive more deeply to prevent treating the symptoms rather than the actual cause. The goal here is to eliminate the problem from ever reoccurring.

- ***A3/A4***
  - *General definition*: A thinking and communication tool; also, a single-page summary or "story" format that ensures logical problem solving.
  - *Broader meaning*: Literally, A3 refers to an 11 × 17 paper size (A4 is 8.5 × 11). More importantly, it refers to a single-page summary (think storyboard) of a problem to be solved. It can also be used to update status and make proposals; it also has other uses. It is primarily a *thinking tool*. Learn this deeply! If you only do one thing to transform your organization, this should be it. It will change your life!
- ***Catch Ball***
  - *General definition*: A deliberate process of communicating up, down and sideways in an organization.
  - *Broader meaning*: This is a critical element of Nemawashi. It requires that all relevant stakeholders in a policy, product or other decision to be undertaken with the deliberate consultation of all involved thus enhancing both success and buy-in. Opposite of stone tablets.
- ***Flow***
  - *General definition*: How work moves in a process from beginning to end.
  - *Broader meaning*: The seamless, uninterrupted movement along a process or product in a value stream. You will hear also "One-piece flow" or its antithesis, "Batching". Here's an easy way to understand it: batching is an elevator; one-piece flow is an escalator.
- **Flow Cell/U Cell**
  - *General definition*: A schematic of workflow within a typical small group or individual work configuration; workflows in a U-shaped pattern allowing a single person or small team to maximize efficiency.
  - *Broader meaning*: U cell or Flow cells are specific workplace layouts that are designed to minimize wasted motion and enhance visibility into work processes while maximizing worker productivity.

- ***Gemba***
  - *General definition*: The actual workplace where real work gets done.
  - *Broader meaning*: The physical place (think shop floor) where *value* (to the customer) is created. Like an exam room for a physician.
- **Hansei**
  - *General definition*: Self-reflection; deep introspection.
  - *Broader meaning*: This is a very much misunderstood concept. It is often defined very superficially as the debriefing, lessons learned or the 'spreading' step of a project. The deeper meaning is to *learn individually*, privately and introspectively, especially as a leader, by asking ourselves honestly, *What could I* personally *have done differently? Where have I failed? What should I do next time? With whom should I share my learnings?*
- **Heijunka**
  - *General definition*: Smoothing of demand to reduce or eliminate peaks and valleys of production, effort or delivery.
  - *Broader meaning*: This is another key concept. It refers to leveling the input, effort and output to ensure relatively even workloads, deliveries, transportation, etc.
- **Hoshin Kanri**
  - *General definition*: Policy Deployment.
  - *Broader meaning*: Hoshins (policies) are essentially strategies and goals that are cascaded down but with particular attention paid to *bottom-up* feedback to surface potential issues and concerns. Most Hoshins are deliberately vague (e.g., "to modernize"). This allows others to align with that general direction while adapting it to their unique circumstances. See also "Catch Ball".
- ***Jidoka***
  - *General definition*: Building in quality at the source.
  - *Broader meaning*: A broad term meaning to ensure that what is being created is error free and does NOT rely on downstream QA inspection or at the end of the line, but rather at each point along the way. Think preventing rework by catching errors before they leave an individual work cycle.
- ***Just in Time (JIT)***
  - *General definition*: Producing work when, where and where it is needed without delay or inventory.
  - *Broader meaning*: JIT is a fundamental concept that differentiates lean from traditional production methods. It seeks to minimize

in-process effort or inventory at any point in the production process; using only what is needed in the exact amount at exactly the right place. No more, no less.

- ***Kaizen***
  - *General definition*: Continuous improvement.
  - *Broader meaning*: This is a core principle. The notion is that you are NEVER perfect but are ALWAYS striving for perfection. Kaizen is a mindset, not a tool.
- **Kamishibai**
  - *General definition*: A visual system of showing when repeatable, routine actions have been made. Example: Red or green colors are used to denote whether a maintenance procedure has been accomplished.
  - *Broader meaning*: The term 'Kamishibai' refers to a person, a storyteller, who would travel from village to village telling a story using wooden panels like in cartoons. The concept was adapted by Toyota to show 'story' of how ongoing work is being completed in a visual way, at a glance, requiring little or no further explanation.
- ***Kanban***
  - *General definition*: Sign card or sign board.
  - *Broader meaning*: It is a visual depiction of what is needed, which includes the relevant reorder information for that item. Kanban can also be a space where things belong, like an outline on the floor where the trash bin goes. A common use is a "production kanban", where workers signal when they are ready for their upstream workers' output. Think of the *time-to-reorder* cards you see on grocery store shelves.
- **Kata**
  - *General definition*: A set of questions designed to help encourage thinking, decision-making and problem-solving skills and team development to push capability to the lowest organizational level possible.
  - *Broader meaning*: Taken from the realm of martial arts, kata is a set of repeatable habits one practices until they become second nature. These are open ended, Socratic questions that help foster a culture of empowerment through the development of deep-thinking routines. They also serve as the foundation for coaching and development efforts.

- ***Muda***
  - *General definition*: Waste.
  - *Broader meaning*: Generally, any work or activity that does not add value to the form, fit or function of a product or service. Eight forms of Muda are commonly referred to. See also, non-value-added (NVA) work.
    - Transportation/conveyance
    - Rework/correction
    - Inventory
    - Motion
    - Over-production
    - Over-processing
    - Defects
    - Unused human capability
- **Mura**
  - *General definition*: Unevenness.
  - *Broader meaning*: A term meaning to uncover things that interrupt and inhibit smooth flow.
- **Muri**
  - *General definition*: Over-burden.
  - *Broader meaning*: Requiring one step, machine or person in a process to work significantly longer or harder than others in the same work stream.
- ***Nemawashi***
  - *General definition*: Consensus building.
  - *Broader meaning*: In US slang, we use expressions like "greasing the skids" to convey this same idea. Nemawashi is derived from an agricultural term meaning "binding up of the roots" (having to do with minimizing the shock of transplanting a tree). Basically, it refers to ensuring that all stakeholders (or roots) have been fully included, informed, advised and consulted on changes that affect them. Think of it as the equivalent of *the best surprise is no surprise* applied to business. While often a time-consuming process, Nemawashi ultimately results in faster overall execution once the stakeholders are all "on the same page".
- ***Non-Value-Added Work***
  - *General definition*: Work that does not directly benefit a customer and which is normally not billable.
  - *Broader meaning*: Some work is NVA but necessary (e.g., housekeeping, maintenance, budget meetings, etc.). But it is work that must be done. Technically, NVA is waste from the customers' vantage point. The organization should strive to separate

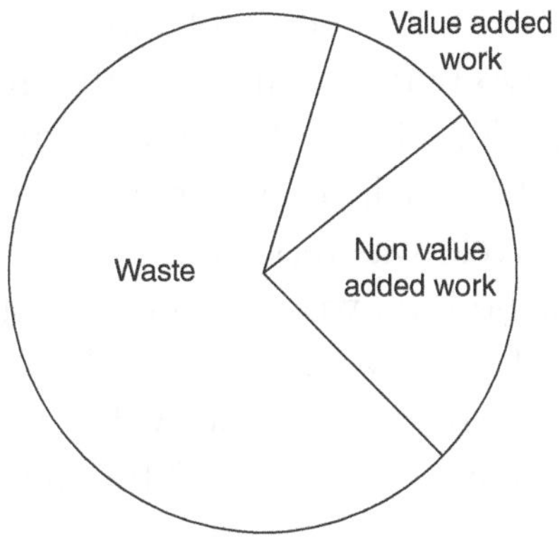

Figure 4.1

it from actual waste so that the waste can then, by definition, be eliminated altogether if possible. An easy way to think about it is that value-added work is that which the customer is willing to pay for. Everything else is either NVA work or waste.

Note: In Figure 4.1, you can readily see the approximate "normal" distribution of work. We like to think that most of our efforts are value added, but rarely is that the case. Normally a tiny fraction of all work adds value. A lot of effort is in the 'non-value-added' but necessary slice. It is indeed waste from the customer's perspective but, since it must be done, it should be treated separately. Clearly, most of the work is waste. Here's an example.

Imagine that you are hosting a Thanksgiving dinner at your home. The actual moment from the time the guests arrive to their departure is generally considered value added from THEIR perspective.

But, from your perspective, a lot of other work is required that will probably be unseen, and dare I say it, unappreciated by your guests. Beforehand there is the making of the list, shopping, the invitations, setting the table, polishing the silver and the cooking, and in the aftermath, there is the cleanup and resetting to 'normal'. All of these are examples of NVA. Again, this is normal and unavoidable but NOT of value to the 'customer'.

Story Time: *How Much of Your Job Is Waste?*

I was attending TPS training at the NUMMI plant on this topic. The instructor suddenly and without notice said, "Follow me!" to the class. He led us from the classroom into the plant. He walked up to a worker who was operating a huge hydraulic stamping machine.

The worker's job was to slide sheet steel squares from a stack on his left into the machine, press two buttons, and then the machine would instantly stamp out a fender with a loud bang. The worker then moved the newly stamped fender into another stack on his right to be moved on to the production line, and the cycle was repeated.

Our instructor approached the worker without notice and asked in a loud voice, "How much of your work is value added?" Imagine the poor guy, suddenly being asked such a question with a bunch of people in ties watching over him. "Ah, maybe 50 percent?" he guessed, pulling out his earplugs.

The instructor, visibly irritated, then said, "No. Your job is 100 percent waste! Only the instant in time that the press is actually shaping the steel is value added. All else is waste!" he exclaimed. Awkward to be sure but the point was made very clearly.

So, back to our waste wheel pie chart, let's look deeper into waste. See the Muda section and make the connections for all the various types of waste involved in this simple example. MOST of your efforts will fall into the waste category.

- **Poka Yoke**
  - *General definition*: A physical, mechanical device or electronic block meant to prevent errors.
  - *Broader meaning*: The goal here is to prevent errors. Think three-prong plug and you have the idea. It's hard to do it wrong. Also, think about entering credit information into a website for an online purchase. If you enter the wrong credit card information, it blocks you until you input it correctly.
- ***Pull***
  - *General definition*: A demand-based system of production.
  - *Broader meaning*: In its opposite form, push; products are produced as fast as the operator can make them. This builds up inventory (aka work in process or WIP) between steps, on store shelves or in warehouses. On the other hand, in a pull system, operators build only what the next worker actually needs and when they need it. Similarly, products that are 'pushed' into the marketplace can build up excess inventory and result in large-scale, low-priced sales to reduce obsolete products for which there is no demand. Think sell one, build one.

- **Sensei**
  - *General definition*: Revered teacher, coach or subject matter expert (SME).
  - *Broader meaning*: **CAUTION**: This is an often misunderstood term! One should **NEVER** refer to *oneself* as a sensei. **NOTE**: If you ever hear a consultant say, "I am a Sensei", run! This is an honorific term used ONLY to describe *others* who are revered for their knowledge, experience and wisdom. It is often considered offensive to use this term to describe yourself.
- ***Spaghetti Diagram***
  - *General definition*: A tool, usually a drawing or sketch, used to record and identify wasted motion.
  - *Broader meaning*: This is often used in connection with 5S work. It is a depiction of how people or products move about in a workspace. A pencil drawing traces the steps of operators continuously over a specified time period. Often different colors are used to differentiate between various operators or to distinguish between different processes occurring in the same physical space. Habitual patterns of movement quickly emerge that can be used as a baseline for improvements in workspace layout, equipment/furniture placement, tool storage, files, standard work sequencing, etc.
- ***Standard Work (SW)***
  - *General definition*: A consistent and repeatable way to produce a product or service.
  - *Broader meaning*: This is the very *foundation* of improvement (kaizen). It is Step 1! After all, how can you improve a process that has many variations in how it is to be completed? Five people doing the same work five different ways demands standardization first. What if every barista produced your latte in their own way? Once a process is standardized, improvement opportunities then become obvious. SW is the *current* best known way to do something. Once baselined, SW shows areas of opportunity for improvement. Think recipe.
- **TPM**
  - *General definition*: Total Productive Maintenance.
  - *Broader meaning*: TPM is a methodology to ensure that critical equipment is always maintained in an "operationally ready" state. Rather than complete reliance on the maintenance department, per se, some maintenance can be completed by the machine operators according to standard work requirements. Think elimination of

machine down time. Example: A cashier can replace the roll of paper in the receipt printer without calling for external help.

- ***TPS***
  - *General definition*: Toyota Production System.
  - *Broader meaning*: Generally thought of as the genesis of the global lean movement and efficiency standard practices that have now gone beyond manufacturing into all industries and endeavors.
- **True North**
  - *General definition*: An articulation of the ultimate direction and sometimes the destination of an enterprise. Similar in nature to a mission or vision statement but broader in scope.
  - *Broader meaning*: These are usually extremely high level, perhaps lofty ambitions, that are unlikely to change from year to year. Think 'Zero Harm' in healthcare environments or 'Zero Defects' in production work.
- ***Value Stream***
  - *General definition*: The complete set of processes that work together to produce a product or service of value to a customer.
  - *Broader meaning*: The combination of all the steps that, taken together end-to-end, transform raw materials into a finished product. More on Value Streams coming up.
- ***Value Stream Analysis or VSA***
  - *General definition*: The process of analyzing all the process steps in a value stream to distinguish between steps that are value added, non-value added and waste. Usually done by a team comprised of all relevant stakeholders.
  - *Broader meaning*: This is a visual depiction of how work is performed. It is like a flowchart but different in that it isolates where value is created and where waste and NVA work occurs. Key term to know! One of the most important things you can do! Very often a starting point for improvement (lean) initiatives.
- ***Visual Management***
  - *General definition*: Seeing and understanding instantaneously what is happening, with no explanation required.
  - *Broader meaning*: If you have seen the typical United Way thermometer in a building lobby showing how contributions are progressing, you get the idea. You should be able to understand what is happening in five seconds from five feet away (the 5 × 5 rule). This is another key principle; learn it, demand it and expect it. Think

ultra-simplicity and low tech. This is one of the most fundamental concepts in lean.

- ***WIP***
  - *General definition*: Work in Process/Progress.
  - *Broader meaning*: The accumulation of all the parts or components of a product or service that has been started but is not yet complete. This is work that has begun or component parts that have moved from raw material or inventory phase but are not yet complete.
- **Yokoten**
  - *General definition*: A deliberate step in spreading or sharing learning at the end of a process, experiment, A3 or improvement event.
  - *Broader meaning*: The basic concept is one of learning and sharing regardless of the success or failure of a project or experiment. This is the Check/Act phase of PDCA. It is critical to chronicle and leverage what worked and what didn't work from a formal post-audit review in order to improve over time. The idea is to standardize what worked well and deeply problem solve what didn't. Critical to organizational learning but frequently over-looked or reduced to a shallow, meaningless postmortem.

There are many other terms and abbreviations that are common in this domain, but this will give you a start.

Let's Dig a Little Deeper into Value Streams

A value stream (n) or value stream analysis (v) is a depiction of the way in which a product or service gets delivered to a customer (internal or external). As in the example shown, it often starts out with the work team showing the current state (good, bad and ugly) and reveals waste and opportunity for improvement. Typically, a series of improvements are then depicted on a 'future state' Value Stream side by side. This is the second best way (behind 5S) to launch lean in your organization.

Note: It is similar but not identical to a flowchart.

A value stream is one of the most fundamental building blocks for your lean transformation. It is often your starting place. As the term implies, a value stream is a cycle of work that produces value for your customers, internal or external. A close approximation to value streams is often found in the naming convention of your internal structural components (e.g., sales, production, shipping, HR, quality, etc.). The term value stream is applied to put a finer point on the work going on in each. It is where we isolate the actual key elements within the function that produce something the customer wants.

Hence, a value stream is usually a one-way series of activities that, combined, produce value.

Value Streams and Christmas Lights

An easy way to think about value streams is to use the analogy of a string of Christmas lights.

Each light along the string can be considered as adding value. The wire between them is like NVA work. Nobody looking at your house will say, "Wow, look at those beautiful wires!" They may be necessary to separate and connect the lights but, by themselves, they don't add to the display. Thus, we try to conceal them from view as much as possible. Think behind the scenes paperwork and processing steps.

Similarly, when we first unbox those light strings, we are likely to encounter a tangled mess that needs to be untangled before they can be hung. Also, this is the time when we locate those bulbs that are burnt out. The Value Stream Analysis is like that.

VSAs seek to uncover the tangles, knots and blown bulbs that interfere with the smooth flow of value to your customers. They also serve as an opportunity to separate out truly non-value-added (but necessary) work from waste that can and should be eliminated entirely.

Chapter 5

Common Lean Tools

What follows is a list of commonly used tools that you will see in most lean enterprises, along with a brief explanation of each.

Note: Most tools are easily found on the internet, with samples of each to see how they are used. This is a slightly deeper dive into each than what was offered in Chapter 4, "Lean Speak". Earlier you learned some of the most common terms but without much depth. Some of the terms are also common *tools*. Let's revisit.

The A3

This is another Toyota invention. It is a single-page 'story' most commonly used for problem-solving. The term A3 refers to the size of paper, it is written as (11 × 17). A4 also refers to a paper size, the more common 8.5 × 11 sheet. If you look in the corner of the glass in your typical office printer, you will see both A3 and A4 depicted.

When I was there, A3s were frequently used as it was the largest size of paper that could be faxed. It allowed for a solid understanding of the problem being addressed with minimum words and maximum images like charts, photos, tables, graphs, drawings, etc. This forced both brevity and clarity simultaneously. A huge benefit was also the reduced need for a live conversation, usually requiring a translator, about the problem.

In the earliest days, they were hand drawn for maximum benefit with the limited technology available then. It also permitted much of the story to be shared with minimum need for language translation. A picture is worth a thousand words, right?

Importantly, A3s also guide the critical-thinking process of the author(s). By completing the A3 sequentially, one is guided through the plan, do, check, act (PDCA) cycle in a systematic and quasi-linear way. Often A3s are prepared by teams vs. single individuals. This is very desirable.

However, I often use an A3 privately to guide my own thinking even if it will never see the light of day. Some people just naturally think in a logical, systematic way but, sadly, I'm not one of those people, so the A3 is a crutch that helps me overcome that challenge. Bottom line here is that the A3 is a gift that keeps on giving

Random Thought: The Wit and Genius of Abraham Lincoln

On an occasion, so the story goes, President Lincoln was making a speech. He apologized for its length as he began to speak, "Ladies and Gentlemen, I apologize in advance for the length of this speech. I didn't have time to make it shorter".

There are literally thousands of examples available showing a huge variation in style and sophistication. You will see some with only four or five boxes and I have seen as many as 20. Nowadays, electronic preparation, transmission and communication are preferred by many. My preference is still for simple handwritten A3s with pictures, charts, tables, graphics, stick figures etc., imagine that.

Keep in mind that, like an artist painting on a blank canvas, there are wide variations. Check out samples online and you'll see what I mean. The bottom line is to share your story in a clear and uncluttered way on a single one-sided sheet of paper.

Here are the basic building blocks of the A3.

First let's look at the "big picture" in Figure 5.1a. Here you will see that the author completes each box sequentially as shown by the arrows. Usually, but not always, this is done starting from the heading or title (not shown) first and following the arrows throughout the cycle of the problem-resolution process.

I mentioned above that this is a 'quasi-linear' process. This is because, as we begin to unravel a problem, we may uncover new information that might force a change in the title or even the problem statement itself. Also, it is not

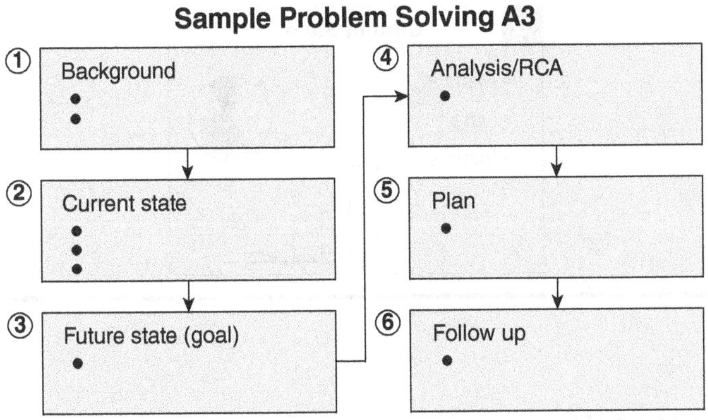

Figure 5.1a

uncommon to start with the future state (aka Target State or Ideal State) and work backwards. This can be quite effective in certain circumstances. Once again, your consultant will guide you.

For now, let's proceed in the more typical linear fashion.

Box 1: Background

In the top left corner of the A3, often referred to as simply "Box 1", you will complete the background in which the problem exists. This enables you to "position" the problem in the proper context. It should be a *short* narrative or, better still, an image showing why you need to address this problem or gap, the business case and why now. This helps your readers (A3 customers) to funnel into where you're going.

Often you will see an "Initial Problem Statement" shown here. For example, you might say, "Due directly to issues with our current hiring process, we have lost several top candidates who took other opportunities during delays in our recruiting process, leaving us to select other, less qualified people as a result". Perfectly legitimate at this point.

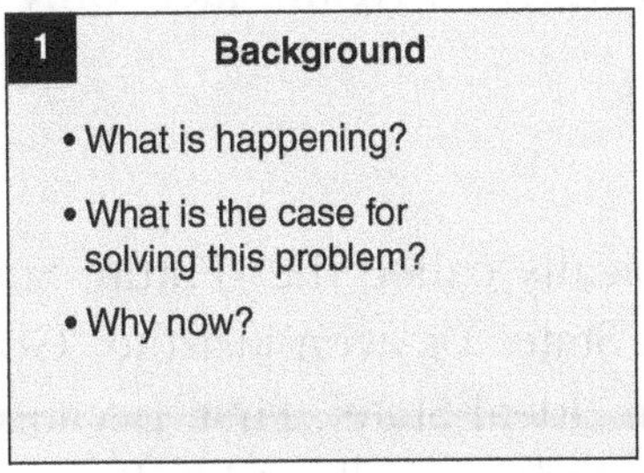

Figure 5.1b

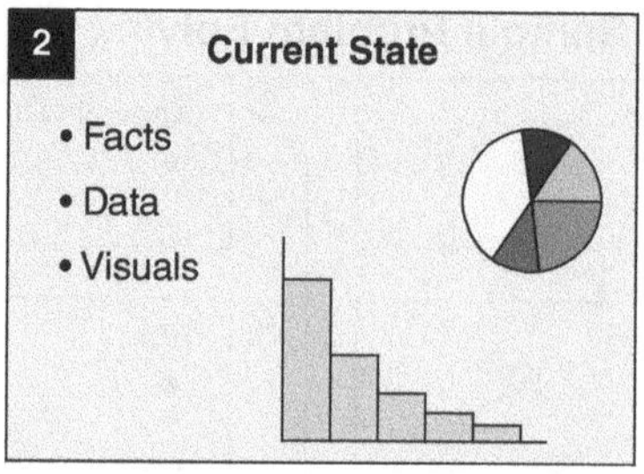

Figure 5.1c

Box 2: Current State

In Box 2 is the Current State (or sometimes Current Conditions) where you will typically see a portrayal of the FACTS and DATA that capture where you are now (see Figure 5.1c). It should explain what is going on in *highly visual* ways such as Pareto charts, sketches, pie charts, etc. Here is where you want to be crystal clear. In the example above, you might show a depiction of the current recruiting process using a process flowchart, a swim lane diagram or an image of the current standard work document. We refer to this part of the process as “grasping the current conditions”.

Note: *Never substitute your opinions here even if you know them to be true!* Here is an example of what *NOT* to write: “Our recruiting process takes too long and is way too complicated”. This is the conclusion you have come to. Maybe the reader will agree, maybe not. But instead, you need to say, “The current recruiting process includes 87 steps and requires 28 days and 12 people to complete before a candidate can be hired”.

Note: If I say, “It’s too hot in here”, I am stating my opinion or, in today’s parlance, “my truth”. Ugh. It is easily refuted by you saying, “No, it’s too cold in here”. Where does that leave us? Who’s right? Better to agree that the current temperature is 65 degrees. Again, facts only here.

Box 3: Future State

Box 3 (Figure 5.1d) is typically called the “Future State”. Acceptable variations include “Target State” or even just the “Goal”. I usually try to discourage using the term “Ideal State”. First, because we rarely know what that even looks like and secondly, it implies some idealized notion of perfection which is normally just a mythical place anyway.

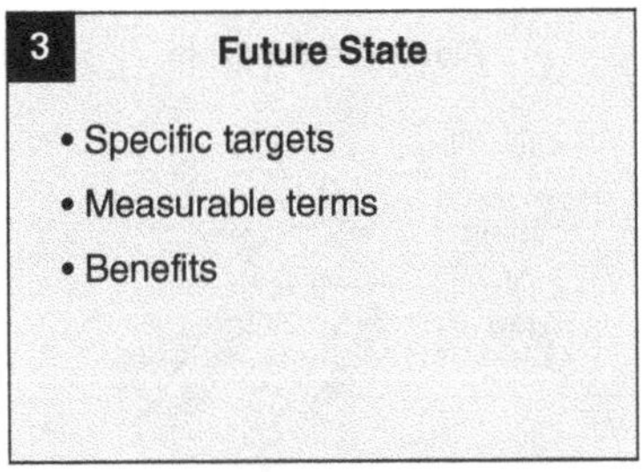

Figure 5.1d

Once again, this is a clear statement of specific targets. In our recruiting example, you might instead say, "Our objective is to reduce the complexity and time-to-hire process to 45 steps or less; to be completed in 14 days or less; by six people or less".

Note: A basic starting point for improvements is VSAs or other kaizen events is usually a 50 percent improvement over the current condition.

Box 4: Analysis

In Figure 5.1e, Box 4, aka "Gap Analysis" or "Root Cause Analysis", is a **KEY** element in lean cultures and one that lean leaders must adopt. When you think about it, most problems tend to be considered "solved" when the symptoms disappear, rather like painting over rust. But on the A3, in the gap analysis, time and care is taken to ensure that you eliminate the problem completely and forever by the elimination of the root cause(s).

There are many problem analysis tools that are useful here. Among them are the Five Whys, Fishbone (Ishikawa) Diagrams, Problem Analysis Trees, QC tools, among others. One of my favorite go-to tools is the Fishbone Diagram. Here's what it looks like.

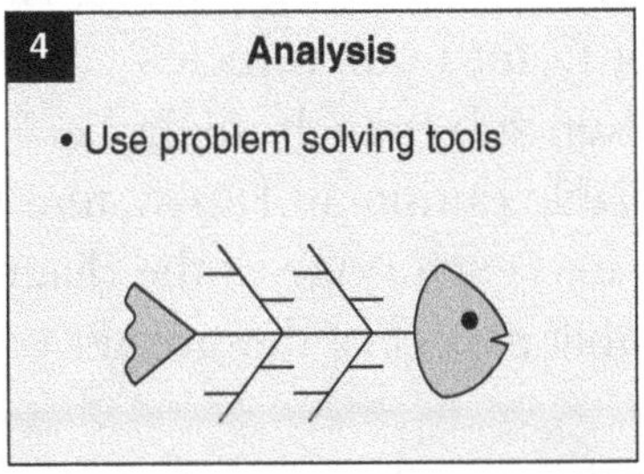

Figure 5.1e

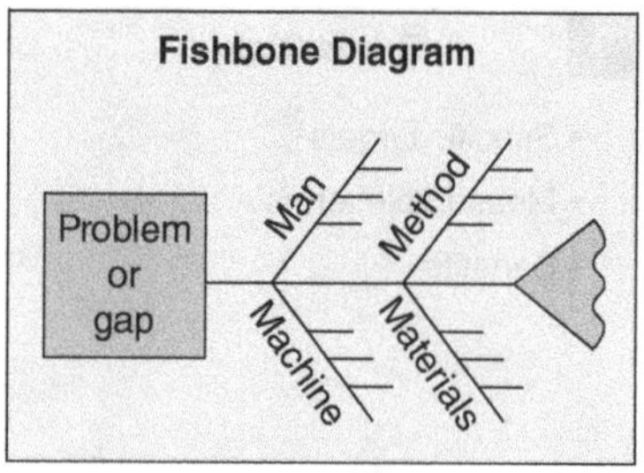

Figure 5.1f

In Figure 5.1f, notice that the problem or gap, shown in the head, is broken down into several 'bones'. Those bones are then further broken down to illuminate the issues you have exposed in your analysis more deeply. Most Fishbone Diagrams will have some form of these basic four M components: *Man* (sometimes *Human* in light of our current cultural enlightenment), *Method*, *Machine* and *Materials*. Frequently, you will also see *Mother Nature* as a fifth M, which allows for physical or natural circumstances, like weather, to be addressed as appropriate to the problem. There is lots of room for variation and customization here though.

Let's Look at Each Bone Separately

(Hu)Man: Here you would break down the elements of the problem or gap according to those factors that are specific to the people involved.

Note: Again, avoid opinions. It is not ok to show here that "Ken is slow" as a key factor in the problem. We always assume that, *given the right circumstances*, everyone will be successful, even Ken. No really.

However, we might appropriately say, "Ken has not completed his recruiting process certification". This is a legitimate fact-based statement. Other human considerations might be appropriate factors to call out here to break the problem down more fully. Example: A person whose height exceeds eight feet will not fit into our vehicles.

An example under the Ken sub-branch might be, "The recruiting certification process is currently unavailable during an HQ system level VSA". The point here is to be able to dig deeper into each bone of the diagram to try to decipher additional facts to support that aspect of the greater problem to be solved.

Method: Here we examine the 'how' as it relates to the problem. An example here might be that no standard work is currently available. We might also call out the procedures that must be followed that may have a bearing on the problem. An example in recruiting might be a depiction of the signature authorization process to approve the request for a new position.

Machine (aka "Systems"): In this branch, we isolate those elements of the problem that come from non-human, mechanical or electronic equipment. Example: "The online requisition approval system is currently being upgraded and is currently unavailable, forcing delays and reliance on manual backup systems".

Materials: As it sounds, these are the things required to perform work such as tools, manuals, etc. So, you might see here, "The recruiting certification test is obsolete and has not yet been updated".

Note: Sometimes you will see an element that could fit under more than one bone. An example here might be Standard Work artifacts. They could be included under either Method or Materials. This is gold! When you find the same thing popping up in different parts of the diagram, circle them and connect them with a line. This may be a hint at a good place to investigate possible countermeasures.

To conclude the Analysis box, this is where you should finally be able to isolate one or more root causes that, if eliminated, will solve your problem permanently.

Note: This is a good time to review your initial problem statement. Having located the major causes of the problem, you may be in a better position to restate your real problem or even the A3 Theme (title).

Box 5: Proposal

This is also commonly known as the Plan or Countermeasures box (Figure 5.1g). This is where you get to finally create your solution(s) to the

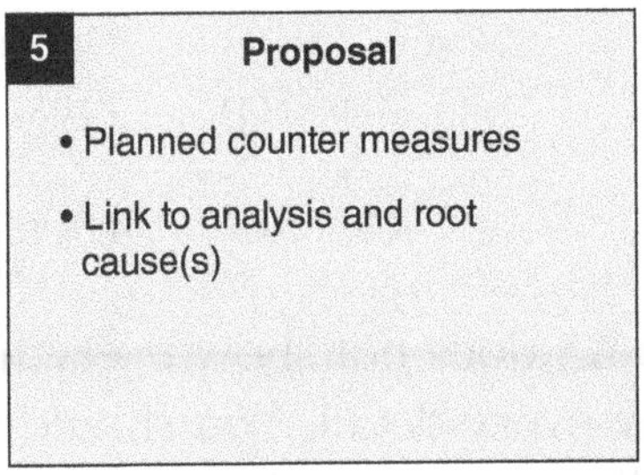

Figure 5.1g

problem at hand. This is very straightforward. As you would expect, your countermeasure should attack the root cause of your problem directly. Precision is required here as much as possible.

Note: Beware of the extremely common and very tempting trap to start with solutions and work backwards on the A3. This is a perversion of A3 thinking! We call it, "a solution in search of a problem". One way to prevent this from happening is to keep a running log of "potential solutions" to consider when you eventually do get to Box 6. This way the ideas won't be lost, but, if you remain true to the process, you will be amazed at how well it works!

By the way, I wince when I see statements in Box 5 like, "We will study the option of outsourcing recruiting". Studying is not a countermeasure. Better to have already done that and state, "Experiment for six months using ACME Outsourcing Company's recruiting software that is designed to work with our existing HR platform". Ah, now we're getting somewhere.

Box 6: Plan

This part (Figure 5.1h) is straightforward. It should show the what, who and when to implement your countermeasure(s). It is common to see some form of project management tool such as a Gantt chart here. Keep it simple and, for purposes of the A3, high level. Sometimes a few simply stated project phases is enough.

Example

Phase 1: Contract with ACME:	Jan–Feb	Lead: Susan, Purchasing Manager
Phase 2: Train staff to use system:	Feb–Mar	Lead: TBD HR Training Department
Phase 3: System Trial:	Mar–Sep	Felix, Lead HR Recruiting Manager
Phase 4: System review, report, recommend:	Oct–Nov	HR team and executive team

Note: Remember that the A3 does not show everything you know about the problem. Nor does it show every detail. You should be ready to share those if asked but it is not usually appropriate here.

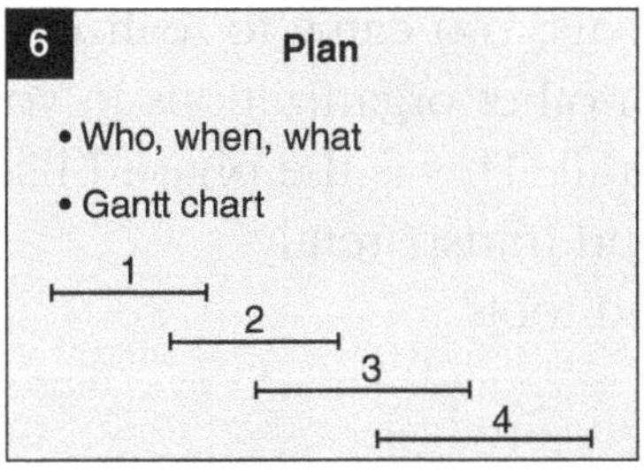

Figure 5.1h

Box 7: Follow-Up

Figure 5.1i is also known sometimes as the Hansei box. This, in my humble opinion, is the most important box of all, why? This is where team and even organizational learning happens. This is where we reflect on our problem-solving work and think deeply about it. This is the time in PDCA, when we capture and standardize those things that worked well so we can repeat them. This is where we may surface any remaining issues or gaps to be solved in another A3 cycle.

We also capture what didn't work as well and problem-solve those things before we start on the next A3, even if it is on an unrelated subject! Often, these reflections are done before a large audience to maximize the benefits of the work, recognize the efforts of the team and share our learning, including failures and mistakes, across the organization.

It is not uncommon to see a follow-up A3 or a deeper dive "Baby A3", on the same topic. You might even see a new arrow going from Box 7 back to Box 1. For example, let's say you have closed out your recruiting experiment with ACME. In the follow-up phase you might discover that, while it improved the process for your organization, it may have caused new problems that you didn't anticipate. You might have found that, even though

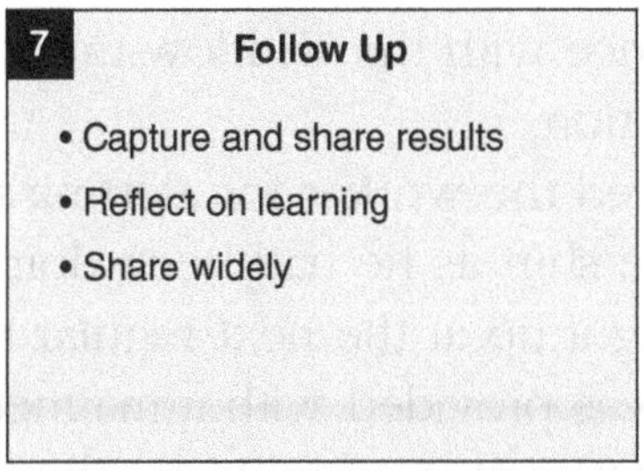

Figure 5.1i

you accomplished your goals, you came to realize that your new system was no longer compatible with other organizations in your same system and sub-optimized the system overall. This is the phase I like to call "Open Kimono". Share freely, completely and transparently.

Back to commonly used tools.

Andon (Light or Signal Board)

Andon, meaning simply 'light', is a visual management tool designed to signal the status of an operation. Different colors mean different things. It is also used to trigger a response by a lead person or supervisor to assist in resolving an issue to return to normal status.

Often these are also accompanied by a sound or even a melody that workers can hear even if they don't happen to be looking at the visual board at that moment. Related to this is the expression of stopping the line or pulling the cord. Normally, this will kick in a pre-planned and rehearsed response such as the lead person going to the position on the line where the problem occurred.

Story Time: *The Lost Screw*

Upon a visit to one of our production plants, I was observing the assembly process of a vehicle door. The team member frequently pulled the cord above his station that ran the length of the entire production line when he had a problem. His lead responded each time the cord was pulled when it lit the andon and started a music sequence thus signaling that help was needed and where.

The issue the operator was dealing with was that he kept dropping screws into the cavity of the door requiring him to try to fish them out before proceeding with the installation. Failure to do so would result in rattles, potential interference with the window-raising mechanism and reduced customer satisfaction.

The lead person thanked the worker for alerting her and told him to continue to the end of the shift as he had been doing as a *temporary countermeasure* and bring it up at the next regular team meeting, which were held each day. He was provided with a magnet on the end of a flexible rod to help. The operator was also asked to be thinking about what was happening and what he thought might be the root cause of the problem.

At the end of the shift, he brought up the issue with his teammates in their routine, daily, collective problem-solving kaizen session. As his lead person had coached him to do, he had thought about finding the root cause of the issue. He felt that he was dropping the screws into the door cavity because they were very small, and his safety gloves were too bulky and not designed for that type of small part.

The team encouraged him to conduct an experiment on his next shift using a different, thinner safety glove that would give him a better feel of the small screw. The next shift resulted in no dropped or lost screws and no need to pull the cord! The team then passed the word across the plant about what they had learned just in case there were other areas experiencing the same or similar problems. Remember: A rising tide raises all boats.

History Lesson

The idea of pulling the cord came from Japanese staff visiting the United States in the early 1950s and traveling by city bus. They noticed that the passengers pulled the cord overhead to set off a buzzer by the driver to alert him that they wanted to get off at the next stop. The cord was not connected to the brakes! It served only to alert the driver to stop at the next SCHEDULED bus stop.

This is exactly how the cord functions in a Toyota production line. It does NOT actually stop the line, but, unless it is cancelled out with another pull, the line will stop automatically at the next appropriate point. It will stay stopped until the problem has been corrected and then the line starts up again.

Note: Line stoppages are routine. Sometimes literally thousands of times a day, especially when a new model is being introduced. During those stops, the operators use the time for routine maintenance, stretching, housekeeping, etc., until it starts up again. Stopping the line as a routine ensures that defects are resolved before the line restarts and prevents the defect from being buried in the build and MUCH harder to resolve later.

Therefore, 'problem consciousness' is constantly being reinforced. As Ohno once said, "The absence of a problem is a problem". Problems are not cause for panic at Toyota. They are considered part of the process and opportunities to learn and improve.

Poka Yoke

Poka Yoke are usually simple devices designed to prevent defects. Ideally, they make it virtually impossible to make an error. This is a great way to engage workers in problem-solving. After a defect or problem occurs, ask the team to try to figure out the root cause and to design a method to prevent it from reoccurring. See also "Five Why's Root Cause Analysis" in Chapter 4, "Lean Speak".

Story Time: *How Did This Happen?*

I was participating in a particularly challenging kaizen team project that took weeks to resolve. The issue was on the production line that surface scratches were occurring on the paint of the top of the right front fenders on a seemingly random basis. Here's where it got weird.

They noticed that the scratches were only on dark colors; they occurred in spurts with no scratches for a several shifts then a bunch all at once. Each car had to be repainted before it could be shipped. The team followed along the production line to what is known as the point of cause or POC.

Note: This is sometimes done backwards from the end of the line to the beginning.

They followed each relevant step … no scratch, no scratch, no scratch, scratch! They had at last found what appeared to be the location on the line where the dark car scratches had been occurring. It turns out that there was an operation having to do with the installation of the windshield. During that process, two operators leaned over and reached across the fender using an overhead tool to align and attach the windshield.

The fenders were protected from incidental worker contact by a rubber drape. But, as they discovered, if the drape slid out of position, it exposed a small section of unprotected paint! As the kaizen team, along with the operators, zeroed in on the operation and observed it, they made a breakthrough discovery.

They found that if, on any given day, that specific operator happened to be wearing jeans, the tiny rivet on the pocket could come into contact with the exposed paint and cause the scratch. The operator himself was blissfully unaware that he was causing this issue as he was focused solely on the windshield installation work.

Most companies would simply have banned the wearing of jeans and/or punished the worker for his "carelessness", not Toyota. The team reassembled to work through the issue. They decided that team members should be able to wear jeans if they wanted to but were simply asked to put small band aids over the rivets when doing so. This did NOT address the root cause, but it was a practical and *temporary* countermeasure.

Diving deeper into it using the Five Why's technique, they found that that the paint had become exposed due to the slipping drape. Not done yet. Why was it slipping? After many uses of the drape, the stickiness of the rubber wore off, allowing it to slip more easily. They had reached a point approaching the root cause.

Note: Further five why analysis would have taken them down a dead end path to "why does the rubber lose its stickiness?" This is a good point to go up a notch to where they could solve the problem permanently.

They realized that the fender drape could be easily attached to the adjacent door drape. By connecting and overlapping the two drapes together, they eliminated the potential for exposed paint in that operation permanently and completely.

But one question remained? Why only on dark colors? The team sampled light color cars that were produced under the same conditions, same operator, same shift. They examined the fenders of those lighter cars under a special light and found, sure enough, there were the same scratches, but the existing quality inspection lighting wasn't sufficient to reveal them!

They fixed the drapes; they changed the lighting, and they notified the customers of those vehicles that there might be a nearly invisible scratch on their fenders. The dealers then repaired them at no cost! The last step, called Yokoten, involved initiating and sharing a summary report of their improvement work on an A3 with all the other manufacturing plants *worldwide*. All this work was done by the actual production workers with coaching by their lead staff and supervisors.

This is how real organizational learning takes place. Keep in mind that most companies would have just hired a painter to touch up as necessary and move on. Not Toyota.

Kamishibai Boards

Another visual management tool to show status of a process. Red or green reversible cards are used to show when a task has been completed.

5S

5S is a continuous process but can also be considered a tool to ensure a clean and safe workplace. Sometimes you'll hear "6S". The extra "S" is for safety.

Note: 5S is a great way to *introduce* lean into an organization or unit. It's simple and creates a quick win that produces a positive buzz. Others see what is happening and want 5S in their areas too. TIP: Start here! This is many people's best experience in lean. Have fun with it! Contests, pictures, stories, etc., are all fair game.

Standard Work

Standard work (SW) comes in many forms. Think of an airliner takeoff checklist. It ensures that required steps are taken in the correct sequence by the correct people at the correct time without reliance on memory. By eliminating variation this way, it becomes the foundation of improvement!

Note: SW is considered the best-known way to do the work TODAY, but it is expected that further improvement is needed. *Standard does not equal permanent*! Think Etch-a-Sketch SW!

X Matrix

On a single page, the X Matrix shows the *alignment* of short-, medium- and long-term objectives of an organization. It's used to ensure strategic alignment and accountability up, down and sideways. By doing so, it also sheds light on work that is NOT aligned and thus should be challenged.

Note: While this is a more advanced lean tool, it is an important one for executives to be familiar with. Done well, it can eliminate a lot of NVA activity and reduce the 'who's on first?' phenomenon. See also, Hoshin Kanri.

Spaghetti Diagram

A spaghetti diagram (Figure 5.2) is a depiction of how people and products move about a given workspace. The black lines shown here are made by following a person or product around continuously for a period to uncover patterns of movement.

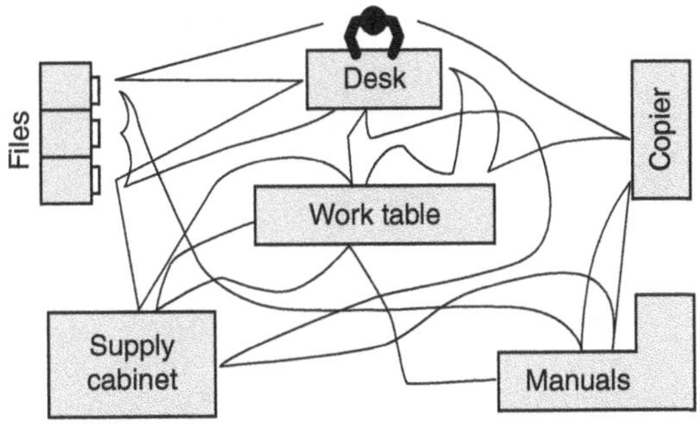

Figure 5.2

This is an extremely valuable tool to support flow and 5S work, as it informs about how to best position machines, tools, furniture, offices, etc., to minimize waste, in this case, motion.

Chapter 6

The Two Pillars of a Lean Culture

If there is anywhere in this book that you as a leader should pay particular attention, it is here. As an executive, you not only represent the culture of your organization, but you also embody it. Your teams will look to you and to the example you set to gauge whether this lean culture thing is for real. Any logical person who has been in the workforce for more than 10 minutes has learned to be cynical and skeptical.

You will hear the question asked (even though it's not really a question but rather a statement), "Is this the flavor-of-the-month?" We have all seen every form of management panacea come down the pike. For example, we have seen management by objective (MBO), Balanced Scorecards, Six Sigma, total quality management (TQM), Quality Circles, etc., etc. Most have come and gone. Some, like Six Sigma, are on life support. The funny thing, though, is that they all started out as being the guaranteed antidote to the flavor-of-the-month! Is it any wonder that people are cynical and suspicious?

Here's a response that I find helps people overcome, albeit slightly, their learned resistance and cynicism. I liken all the above to fad diets that come and go. We have seen the grapefruit diet, Atkins, South Beach, Mediterranean, The Zone, Paleo diets, etc., fade in and out. The number of diet supplements available is endless, too.

But if you read the fine print closely on *all* of them, they all say something like, "Taken along with proper diet and exercise". So, here's the question. What if we just stuck to proper nutrition and exercised, would we still need any of this stuff in the first place?

This is where lean comes in. You can explain it as the company's 'fitness' program. Lean is all about positive habits that are practiced every single day all over the place. This approach generally resonates with people in terms they can understand and relate to. It will not eliminate their skepticism altogether, but it might buy you some time to demonstrate that this thing has staying power because it is simply NOT a fad any more than brushing your teeth is a fad.

There are two transcendent pillars that I would offer for your consideration borrowed shamelessly from Toyota. These two pillars are timeless and will support your entire culture.

Pillar #1: Respect for People!

Without this commodity present, you have my permission to stop right now. Save yourself from further reading, research, consultants, etc. Don't waste another dime on it. You will never truly make lean work in your company, why? To fully understand the importance of this is to understand the relationship between soil and seeds. You must cultivate a culture of respect BEFORE planting lean. As simple as it sounds, this fundamental notion is the single biggest reason why most lean transformations fail. Cultural preparations—tilling the soil if you will—is critical before planting lean.

This idea of respect for people goes beyond simple courtesies like calling people Mr. or Ms. It goes way deeper than superficial recognition and appreciation programs that any civilized organization employs nowadays anyway.

True respect gets at the idea of understanding and treasuring the individuals on your team as the individual humans they are and seeking to create an environment where people can, as I like to say, "Be that person that our Creator made, every single day!"

Random Thought

I am going to go out on a limb here and say that, for many leaders, we take more personal responsibility for the care and feeding of our house plants than we do our team members. "*What did he just say?*" Before you throw this book out the window and blast me on Yelp, allow me to defend such a provocative statement.

We tend to equate fairness with equality. You know that watering a plant is good for it. Therefore, you would treat all of the various plants you own exactly the same way, right? You would water the cactus, the ivy, and the ferns the same amount at the same time because it's important that they are treated 'equally'. All the plants would get the same exposure to the sun and identical pots to grow in. Let's just treat them all the same!

If you do that, chances are that while some may thrive, others may wilt and die. What happened? You treated them all the same!

So back to my premise, you would probably agree that each plant has its own unique requirements to thrive. It says exactly what those requirements are, for each type of plant, on the plastic stake that came stuck in the soil when you bought it. Failure to treat them according to those care and feeding instructions will probably not turn out well. But, if they do die on you, it's reasonable for you to ask yourself if you followed those instructions. If not, you are more likely to accept the responsibility that you killed them than you are to blame the damn plant for dying!

Here's the problem. Our team members don't have little plastic 'care and feeding' stakes stuck in their belts. We risk some of them wilting if we treat them all the same, don't we? The trouble is that they are NOT all the same. Treating them *equally* might be harmful to them compared to others. Some are quite content to be planted in a small pot and sit on the desk next to you. Others need big planters and like it next to the windows.

It's better to be 'fair' with them. Fairness is capturing whatever information you can about each and every one of them individually to help you figure out how they need to be cared for. That way each has a much better chance of growing to their full height, as a species. A cactus will never reach the heights of a redwood but, with proper care, it will grow the best it can. It will be limited only by its unique DNA and the conditions that are present around it. Make sense?

Random Thought: On Blue-Footed Boobies and Flying Fish

A flying fish is not a bird. But it has evolved so that it can fling itself out of the water just long enough and far enough to avoid being eaten. Ditto for the Blue-Footed Boobie. It is not a fish but, in order to survive, has learned to 'swim' underwater long enough to catch a fish and, hopefully, make it back out before he runs out of air.

We are like that in some ways. We try to adapt to conditions that aren't really natural for us. For example, I am not good at things like financial data analysis. Not my thing. But, if it pays well enough, I can try my best to adapt to it. I will never achieve excellence and I might hate it but I will fake it as long as possible to keep my fat salary coming.

Let's Look at This Another Way ...

I appreciate antiques. I recognize that they are not always symmetrical, sturdy, flawless and bullet proof. I acknowledge that they are frail sometimes and might require special care. Each piece has its own story. That story is told in the cracks, worm holes and initials carved on them from their previous 'life' before I came along. It is not that I appreciate them despite their flaws, but because of them! After all, that's the 'character' I was looking for when I bought them.

Approach your people with that same level of curiosity and genuine appreciation of them as unique people who have been shaped simply by their experiences in life. Yes, we all get a little weird over time. A true culture of respect accepts that fact and seeks to leverage the sum total of what we have each become. It is to treasure and, yes, to leverage each individual's talents and life experiences.

Story Time: *The Lone Cypress*

Along the west coast of California there is the famous scenic 17-mile drive along coastal Highway 1. This is home to some of the most spectacular and iconic scenery in all the land. Approaching Pebble Beach there is the equally famous Lone Cypress tree. It has been photographed and chronicled by countless photographers over the decades.

As you approach it from any direction, there are signs reading, "5 miles to the Lone Cypress", "1 mile to the Lone Cypress", "Parking for the Lone Cypress" and so on. So, what's the big deal? It's just a tree growing on a granite outcropping all by itself. Yet, oddly, it seems everybody wants to be seen next to it.

Lovers take selfies in front of it. People drive miles out of their way just to say they have seen it. It is featured on countless calendars, paintings and postcards. Google it and you'll see what I mean.

But why? The big deal of course is that the tree exists at ALL; it is somewhat miraculous. It sits there clinging to a rock. No other trees around to shield it from the incessant winds and Pacific storms. There is no apparent freshwater source to nourish it. It survives even the legendary California droughts. Yet somehow, it exists.

As a tree, outside the context of this magnificent backdrop, nobody would want it in their yard. It's distorted, asymmetrical, half dead and scruffy. But what makes it so special is that it has survived despite what people and nature have done to it. Nothing seems to be able to kill it. Personally, I think it would make a perfectly good picnic table. Maybe a fence. But that's just me.

So, what does this have to do with respect, you ask? Each of us is in some way distorted, too. Life has caused us to be less than perfect in stature or symmetry. We all have had experiences that have shaped us into what we are today. So why is there no parking lot for people who just want to see you and me? Why aren't people making pictures of US for calendars and postcards?

I use this metaphor to highlight that deep respect comes from fully appreciating all the things about your people that you are most likely completely ignorant about. What are their stories? Try asking them. You'll be amazed at what you learn about them. And they will love you for it!

To me this is the ultimate form of respect. It is to really know people and to learn to treasure their uniqueness and to honor their life's journey. What would it feel like to work in a place like that? If you can create a culture that respects its people and adapts itself TO them, you will be well on your way to building something special. Something that underpins a true lean culture.

During my career at Toyota, I witnessed something extraordinary like this. I saw jobs being shaped around the individual and their unique strengths, not the other way around. Common sense really. We all know the idioms like, "He's a square peg in a round hole" or "She's a fish out of water" or "so and so is a misfit".

These are clues that mean we already acknowledge this as a problem. What if we could find or create square holes? I ask you, have you ever felt like you were in a role that just *wasn't you*? Most of us would say yes. What does that feel like?

So, to put a finer point on this, your job is to create a culture where people feel like they belong. Like they matter. Like they are succeeding despite their shortcomings and weirdness. A place where it is assumed that they are doing the best they can every day. Where the team talks each other up, covers for each other's flat spots and lifts up each other's morale. A place where people are not set up to fail by putting them in roles that don't fit them.

This isn't boilerplate team building. No pizza party or retreat can create a culture of such deep appreciation! Sorry. If that isn't the case where you are, you should ask, "what is happening that causes my staff to do less than I know they can do? What's holding them back?" Read on.

The Secret Sauce; Discretionary Effort

As you can see in this sketch (Figure 6.1a), all of us are capable of much more than what is normally required to keep our jobs. Some say we can do as little as 40–50 percent of what we are capable of doing and yet still be able to stay out of trouble. The difference between the minimum expectations of my role and my personal maximum (100 percent) capability or potential is *totally discretionary.*

Put another way, if my work is at or above the minimum, you can't make me (or anybody else) do more! You can probably force me to work at least at the minimum, but no more. Anything extra comes from ME! Think DMV. Chances are that if I am consistently at or below the minimum, eventually something will happen.

Here are two common scenarios:

1. Somebody redefines the minimum of my job.
2. I get fired (eventually).

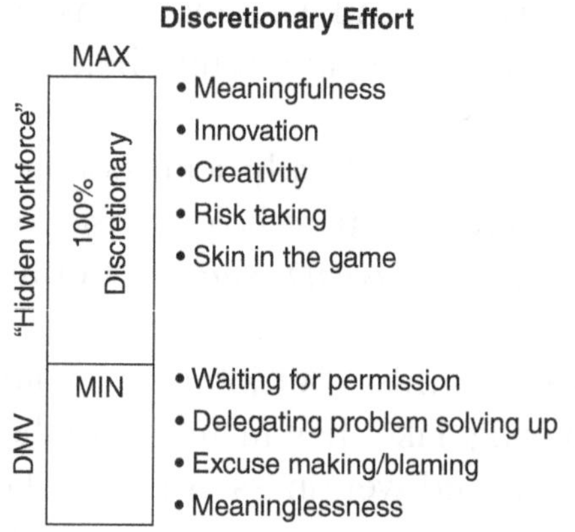

Figure 6.1a

Note: Typically, real minimum expectations are NOT included in job descriptions or postings. They are discovered by being constantly tested, probed and redefined. Your organization's behavior toward these folks really determines how low the minimum really is. So, if Joe gets to keep his job operating at 50 percent of his potential, you can't expect more from Jane, now can you?

In the area above the minimum, we start to see innovation, creativity, risk-taking and skin-in-the-game 'ownership'. The biggest driver of all is meaningfulness.

In the range at or below the minimum, we see people waiting for permission to act, delegating up the chain-of-command, excuse making and finger pointing/blame placing. The biggest restraining force is typically meaninglessness. Take away the meaning of work, take away discretionary effort.

Now let's overlay your team against the discretionary effort band (Figure 6.1b). Chances are you have some folks at the top of the curve who always strive for their best. You are lucky if you have ten percent like this. With you or without you, they are constantly at the front of the pack. Bless them, for they are the movers and shakers.

But, on the bottom end of the bell curve, you are also likely to have another ten percent of people who you can never quite count on… or even find when you need them. You are probably thinking about them now. Maybe they're new and still getting onboarded. More typically though, these are team members that are just not engaged for whatever reasons. God sends them to us because He has a sense of humor, I think.

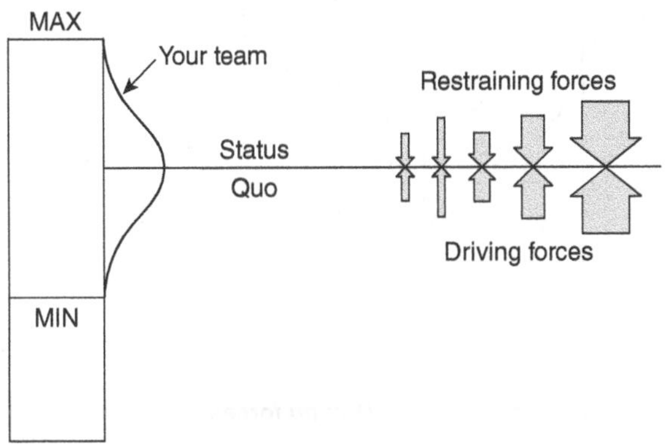

Figure 6.1b

That leaves the bulk of the workforce, let's say 80 percent somewhere in the middle. We might characterize these guys as "competent". They consistently give more than expected but less than they are capable of. Some make an unconscious calculus about how much effort they are willing to put forth. They know that they can keep their jobs by being comfortably above the minimum, but they are holding back that extra effort.

We consider many variables like

- Do I have the tools to do my job?
- Does my boss care about me?
- Do my co-workers appreciate and value me? And the biggie …
- Is there any MEANING to my work? Research has shown that when meaning is present, discretionary effort climbs sharply. Given enough meaning, Herculean effort is possible, exceeding even the maximum we believed we had within us.

If you could drive 20 percent more discretionary effort from any of these three groups, which one would you pick? I'm going with the middle, average group. It's sheer numbers. By virtue of the size of the middle group, you will benefit much more than you would gain by increasing either extreme group by 20 percent. Simple math.

This is called a Force Field Analysis. In Figure 6.1c, you see that there are more-or-less equal and opposite forces at work that serve to maintain the status quo. These forces cancel each other out. Driving forces try to

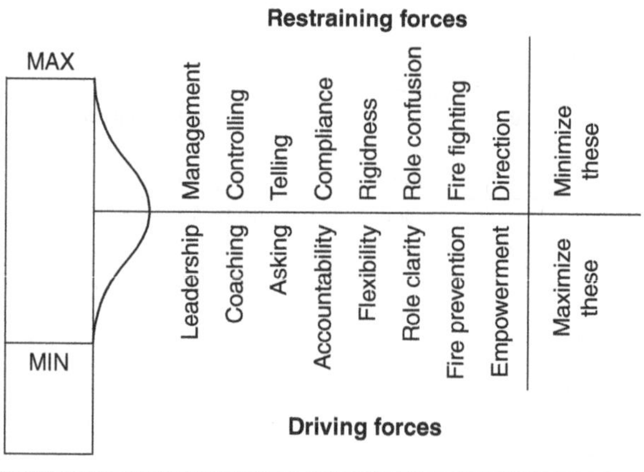

Figure 6.1c

increase deployment of discretionary effort, while Restraining forces have the opposite effect.

In the sketch, you can see some of the possible forces labeled. The trick here, as their leader, is to schedule time for your teams to label these forces in their own areas. Focus on one of the restraining forces and have your team figure out how to eliminate it.

Example: Let's say you have a nursing unit in a hospital and one of the restraining forces they identify is "hunting for supplies". Institute a rigorous 5S process and you will greatly minimize the effect of this negative force! Not magic, common sense!

TIP: Adding driving forces will also have some effect but not nearly as much as eliminating or minimizing restraining forces will have.

Effort vs. Leadership Attention

Let's consider Figure 6.2, here you have the normal distribution of effort spread across your team. But let's also begin to think about how you devote your attention. Chances are that you will be applying more of your time and energy to the two extremes but not so much in the middle, why?

The group at the top end are fun to work with. They are constantly volunteering, making suggestions for improvements and starting new and exciting projects, and their positivity is contagious. They provide the lift in the organization. They are your star performers.

The other end of the curve *requires* your attention. First you have to find them. Then you have to motivate them, usually daily. Then HR gets involved to try to remediate them. They are your poorest performers. You get the idea.

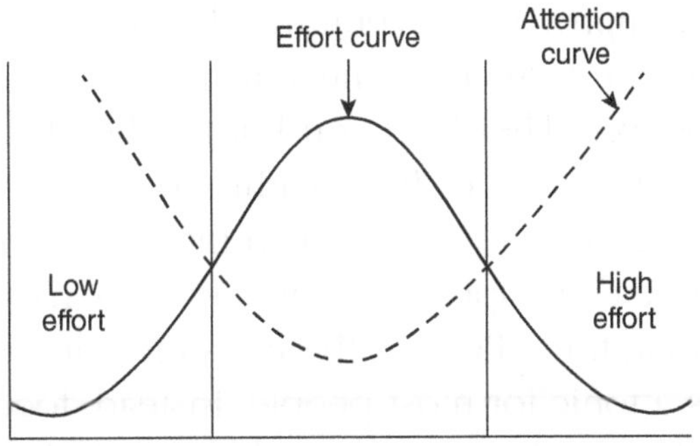

Figure 6.2

Reflection Question: So, What's Left of Your Attention for the Average Workers?

I once asked a group of leaders in a workshop to write down the name, without thinking, of at least one of their best workers, easy. Then I asked to them write down the name of a bottom performer without thinking about it. Again, easy.

Finally, I asked them to write down the name of an average worker, harder. They stumbled here. We tend to overlook these folks. They aren't stars but they aren't slugs either. Regrettably, they have become more or less invisible to us. Put another way, we systematically ignore most of the people, most of the time. Ugh!

Random Thought: The Opposite of Love Is?

Question: *What is the opposite of love?* If you said, *hate,* you would be wrong.

When you consider that the worst form of punishment in prison is NOT what we normally think of as punishment at all. It is isolation. It is apathy. It is indifference. It is being locked away alone; unseen and unheard. It is being cut off from the rest of the world. They call it being put in the "hole". It's a horrible fate, isn't it? In a word, it is to be rendered irrelevant. It makes prisoners crazy. And, in the end, more manageable, too.

We all know that kids insist on our attention, even if it's negative; to them it's better than being ignored, at least. Are we systematically ignoring most of our people? Do they feel irrelevant? Do they think they matter to you? Are we punishing them for being average by being apathetic toward them? Scary to think about.

So, if you want to improve the overall productivity of the whole team, try to ignore your bottom performers as much as possible and leave your top ones to their own devices. They'll let you know when they need something from you. Their motivation comes from within, most likely anyway.

But stay alert for the bottom to do something *approximately right,* like showing up, and be quick to apply your attention. Don't wait for perfection. You'll be waiting a long time. Reward the movement if not the results yet. Just being noticed is a tonic for most people. Instead, focus 80 percent of your time and attention on the average workers. Seek them out. Get to really know them. You'll be surprised at what you'll get.

The Moral of the Story

If you begin to reshape the attention curve to match the actual performance curve more closely, you will be amazed at how much more discretionary effort comes from them simply being noticed by you! Try it.

Story Time: *Hurricane Sandy*

Pay close attention here. This is what discretionary effort looks like.

I recall a haunting image coming from live news coverage shot amid Hurricane Sandy in New York City. As it slammed into New York in the middle of the night, patients were being transferred between hospitals by staff trying to find ways to protect and care for them despite power outages, wind, rain and the like.

One image is permanently etched in my mind. It was a nurse carrying a preemie down a dark emergency exit flight of stairs. She was holding a small flashlight in her teeth, cradling the baby while administering air through a manual respirator. She gently passed the baby to the next caregiver in the stairwell and then went back up the unlit stairway to get the next baby. All this in the middle of the night with horrendous winds and a deluge of rain. Wow! Heroics? Indeed, but it was more than that.

What if, in the middle of this crisis, one nurse glanced at her watch and said something like, "Oh, sorry. My shift is up. Somebody else needs to take this baby"? What we witnessed that night is a wonderful example of how meaning ignites and deploys discretionary effort.

Who knows, that nurse might have been the absolute worst nurse in the hospital under normal conditions, but in that moment, she dug down deep and found something that drove her to achieve real excellence. She might even have shocked herself!

Businesses that employ or, better yet, *ignite* people like this consistently outperform their competitors. Passion is itself a differentiator. Besides, if you have that kind of workforce, you need far less people in the first place. A few passionate people who believe strongly in your mission can lift your entire organization. Especially if those people happen to be execs like you. Just sayin' …

So, what does discretionary effort look like at your place? Would you even recognize it if you saw it? If so, what would you do about it? The good news is that it is something that CAN be bottled. More on that later.

Pillar #2: Continuous Improvement (Kaizen)

Regardless of how good your company or its products or services may be, there is still room for improvement. At least that's the assumption that lean makes. While we use terms like "the pursuit of perfection", we must acknowledge that none of us is even close. Organizations that believe in continuous improvement are constantly striving to achieve the next level.

Look at Apple. No matter how good the initial iPhone was, it has been eclipsed steadily with more and more improvements. Almost every month, a new OS update comes down the pike. Those that rest on their laurels and slip into complacency are eventually overtaken. The dustbin of history is filled with great but complacent and obsolete companies. Think Studebaker.

The real danger, yes danger, is that you either are or you become "the best", *numero uno,* in your industry. Quickly the energy to improve fades away. I love how Avis adopted the slogan, "We try harder" since they were second behind Hertz.

I often ask execs what perfection looks like on the golf course. Eventually, they will say 18. I then add, "Yes, perfection is a score of 18 on every golf course, every day". So even the world's best golfers will never come close. Yet they keep trying because true competitors try to beat their *own* scores even more than beating their competition.

Years ago, there was a Harvard Business Review (HBR) article titled, "No Satisfaction at Toyota". It delved deeply into the heart of the matter. At Toyota there is a constant and urgent sense that, yes, we are good, but we are not good enough. All this despite being the industry leader for decades! Dissatisfaction is their rocket fuel.

After a compliment was paid to a CEO of a major mid-west hospital system, that his hospital was the "best example of lean in healthcare we have seen", he replied, "Well, then I guess that makes us the cream of the crap!" You gotta love it! This is the atmosphere and culture you want to create.

Reflection Questions

- Are your people content with the way things are?
- Is there energy and passion to improve?
- What would it take to ignite that passion?
- Is there a *healthy* level of dissatisfaction present?

Chapter 7

What Key Principles Drive a Lean Culture?

Here are some key principles that have been either clearly articulated and are commonly understood, and some others that are implicit that I have discerned from my own experience and observations over many years.

Key Principle #1: Keep It Simple

While you won't see this particular principle laid out in other books, etc., it is a deeply embedded philosophy that is worth elevating into our consciousness. As I mentioned in the introduction, while I was at Toyota, I learned the real value of simplicity.

I often repeat my personal mantra that the only thing better than low tech is no tech. Don't use a pen when a pencil will do. Don't use a pencil when a crayon will do. You get the idea.

Case in point: A3 thinking and writing should be done by hand, especially in the early draft stages. No fancy graphics or slick PowerPoint slides required. Just the minimum necessary to convey the idea. Often a picture, sketch or chart will suffice.

This is the actual genesis of my "Lean Leadership on a Napkin" series. It is my desire to keep things simple. Simplicity should be prized greatly. Why describe where a tool should go on a wall if a simple outline of the tool on the wall (shadow board) will do? The funny thing is most people will tell you that they agree. But as I mentioned earlier, people will claim that they love simplicity and yet end up making things unnecessarily complex. Why is that?

I suspect that we are still fighting the teachings we learned in elementary school. When we were told we had to write a paper, what was the first thing the students asked? That's right, "How LONG does it have to be?" We were told that it had to be a certain length to qualify for a better grade. In other words, we learned that more is better. I'm guessing that bigger books sell better than smaller ones. If so, I'm in trouble.

Nevertheless, I believe strongly in the axiom, *less is more!* So, if you can instill in your company this same principle, and if you *reward* it, you will start to relieve your organization of some of the weight and clutter that slows it and your people down.

Story Time: *The Power of Simplicity*

I had a friend who left Toyota a year or two before I did. He was a top exec in a major hospital in Southern California. He was responsible for real estate, facilities and construction projects. When I cranked up my consulting business, he hired me to teach A3 writing there. What he told me is representative of what I'm talking about here.

He said that his direct reports would come to him with project proposals some of which were three inches thick! He showed me a stack of them behind his desk that awaited his review and disposition. He asked rhetorically, "Do they really expect me to read and digest all that?"

I did as he asked and taught his team how to write A3 proposals. In one case I remember, there was a proposal to put a large awning over an outside playground in their childcare area. It had been in the queue for *years* pending approval. The project sponsor took my A3 writing workshop. She produced the same proposal on a *single page* and got it approved within a week!

Reflection Questions

- How is complexity influencing your team?
- How can you make things simpler, faster *and* yes, cheaper?
- What is causing delays in project approvals?
- How do people react when they are asked to document their ideas or problems?
- What would happen in your organization if you started to conspicuously reward simplicity?

Key Principle #2: Humility

Humility is a time-honored value learned by most people quite naturally growing up in Japan. The common gesture of bowing is evidence of this. It is therefore not surprising that this value would be perpetuated in their business dealings and exported beyond its borders the way Japanese products are.

We in the United States have from our very beginnings developed quite different values of independence, competition, self-reliance and individuality. All these have served us very well, but certain aspects of leading in a lean culture tend to call us to question how some of these values may either serve us or actually get in our way.

I have arrived at the notion that we cannot just put on humility as we would a coat. One does not necessarily consciously decide, "I'm going to become humble today". I have learned that, when immersed in a true lean culture, humility simply happens.

How is this so? One sub-principle is called a "questioning mind". Edgar Schein, notable author and unquestioned leader in the realm of Socratic coaching, has called it, "Humble Inquiry". He wrote a great book of the same name. Check it out.

If you have young kids at home, you may have tried asking them open-ended (Socratic), probing questions to understand their thought processes. I remember when my daughter was about three, she saw me sweeping the floor and asked, as kids will do, "What are you doing, daddy?" I asked her, "What do you think I'm doing?" She replied, "Brooming". I guess she figured that if one used a broom then it follows naturally that I must therefore be "brooming". When you think about it, it is a perfectly logical extrapolation.

At another time I asked her, "What is inside your head, do you think?" She looked at me incredulously and said, "My brain bone, of course Dad. Duh!" You gotta love it!

Had I never asked these types of questions, I would have missed out on these precious moments and insights into how she thought at the time.

When practiced, this type of *servant leadership* starts with the assumption that people will learn more deeply when they are prompted by answering thoughtful, non-manipulative questions more than they will learn by being told what to do. Truly Socratic questions are framed more from a place of neutral curiosity than from direct scrutiny or judgement questions. You must also be conscious of your tone of voice. Imagine if your boss were to ask you the seemingly innocuous question after you had experienced a failure, "What were you thinking?" Yes, technically it meets the definition of a Socratic question but, depending on the tone or body language, the message might be quite different.

Leaders who practice this skill consistently eventually begin to learn and therefore value the thoughts, ideas, perspectives and instincts of the people they serve. When you think deeply about it, you will conclude that humble people learn more than arrogant ones do. Don't be afraid to overtly acknowledge as you try this out that you are actively TRYING to be a better leader. This will go a long way towards building respect and trust then by just faking it.

Likewise, humble organizations also learn more than arrogant ones do. Humble companies are always looking for ways to improve. They ask questions of their customers and employees and, perhaps more importantly, they listen!

Reflection Questions

- How would you describe yourself on a humble—arrogant scale?
- How would your team rate you? Your business?
- How humble are your subordinate leaders?
- How well do your people think you truly understand them?
- How do your customers perceive you?

Key Principle #3: Zero Defects "Mentality"

I want to inject a possible area of potential confusion or apparent contradiction here at the outset. Zero defects do not equal perfection. It is possible to produce a product with zero defects that nobody wants. Imagine a perfect typewriter. This represents the most serious and fundamental defect of all! No amount of effort will overcome a product or service that nobody wants.

Zero defects is also an aspirational mentality, as is perfect safety. Or in the case of healthcare, zero harm. It is really a statement of our desires and ambitions more than a practical reality. If not zero, then how many defects are OK? These are also sometimes called high level Hoshins. In that way, these aspirational goals become *True North* ambitions rather than monthly or even annual targets.

This is an obsession with legitimate lean enterprises. We don't strive so much for defect elimination because of some extraneous reason; we do it for our customers! Many companies have invested heavily in Six Sigma programs for precisely this reason. As a leader, this is a mindset you must foster everywhere.

	Right	Wrong
Right	RR	RW
Wrong	WR	WW

Figure 7.1a

Of course, we never want to foster a culture of mediocrity. That goes without saying. But we can shift from a long-term aspirational goal to a shorter-term improvement goal, such as reducing lost time injuries by 50 percent in the next year. Think milestones.

Reflection Questions

- What does a defect look like in your business?
- What can be learned from your warranty processes?
- What are your customers telling you?
- What have you gotten used to or accepted as inevitable?
- What level of defects do you tolerate?
- Where can your competitors seize on your vulnerabilities?

The *Right Work/Wrong Work* chart (Figure 7.1a) is a particularly useful tool. It can help guide you to understanding what value there may or may not be in your work. Use it to coach your teams to isolate NVA work, products or services. Let's examine each box individually.

Upper Left Box

Right Work Right (RR): The Golden Zone!

- Your goal is to do the right things in the right way. The right work is, by definition, that which your customer values (tangible and intangible).
- Doing it 'right' means doing it in a way that is efficient and that value flows smoothly to the customer. It is work that meets their needs on the first try without any rework or correction.

Upper Right Box

Right Work Wrong (RW) on the Right Track But Needs Improvement

- This is doing work that the customer values but with room for improvement as to how it is delivered.
- Doing it wrong means that eventually the customer gets what they want but often not on the first try. It may mean that the delivery of that value was awkward, defective or in some way less than a pleasant experience for the customer. Example: Buying a car through a dreadful sales experience.

Lower Left Box

Wrong Work Right (WR): A Trap! Improvements Made Here Are a Wasted Effort

- Wrong work here is work that does not deliver real value to the customer. The product or service does not meet the customer's expectations or needs.
- Doing it right here means that you may have a great experience, but the product or service is inadequate. Example: A painter is a delightful person to work with. He is clean, efficient and reliable, but he paints your house the wrong color. Another example is creating a timely report that is 100 percent accurate that nobody reads. See the story below to illuminate this further.

Lower Right Box

Wrong Work Wrong (WW): STOP NOW! Trash—Poor Quality of No Value

- This is work effort or a product/service that the customer doesn't value, and the experience is unpleasant.
- An example here is creating a product or an experience that is neither what the customer wanted or expected. An example is soliciting door to door that is an annoying experience for a product or service that wasn't requested.

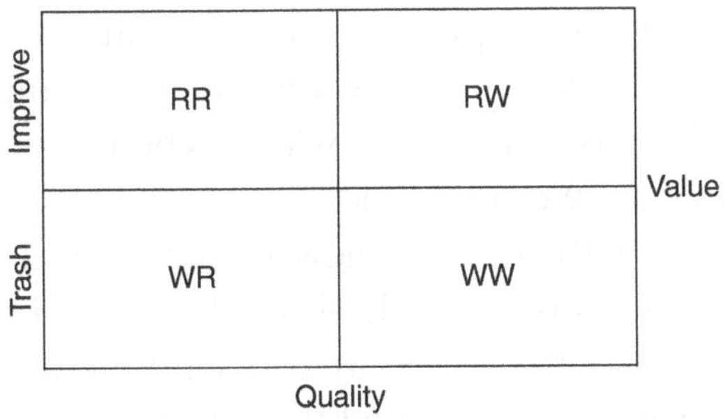

Figure 7.1b

In Figure 7.1b, the horizontal line dividing the upper row (RR and RW) from the lower row (WR and WW) represents value to the customer. Above the line, work is what the customer wants. Below it, the customer does not desire or benefit from the product or service. The goal, of course, is to focus on only work above the horizontal line and delete work below it.

The vertical line dividing the two columns (RR and WR) and (RW and WW) represents the quality of the work. You want to drive your quality towards the top left corner.

Note: It is possible for a piece of work to have all four components at the same time. Imagine receiving a report that contains some of the information that you need and is clear and accurate while other parts of the same report may have errors or contain information that is of no use to you. Here you must dissect the various parts of the work and strive to improve the 'right work' and eliminate the rest. Remember, the customer will tell YOU what they want but you may well have to ask.

Story Time: *Meaningless Pursuit of Perfection*

I was called on by one of my automotive clients to consult with a team that produced a monthly Parts Report. It was a recap of everything to do with parts for the previous month. Their work product was a large four-inch binder broken into many tabs having to do with sales, suppliers, inventories, vendors, warehousing, transportation, obsolescence, supply chain issues, etc.

The team called on me as they had lost a team member to another project and were now trying to streamline the production process of their report with the remaining five members, each responsible for their own sections of it.

As you can now imagine by now, I first asked the team, "Who is your customer?" After an awkward silence, their response was, "We don't actually know". I then asked, "What happens to the report after you are done producing it"? They said, "We put it into the internal company mail system addressed to six mail stops". I followed with, "Where are those mail stops located"? Same response, "We don't know".

I ended the meeting with some homework for them. I asked them to go find out where the mail stops were physically located, go there and ask the team there what they do with the report you send them every month.

A week later we reconvened. I asked them to brief me on what they found. Here was their response:

> We did as you suggested. We were only able to locate four of the six mail stops. We discovered that two of them no longer exist. Nobody knew where they had gone. Even the mailroom couldn't tell us. Mail sent there was apparently just dumped.
>
> We then asked the remaining people at the other four mail stops about who gets the report and what they did with it. All the recipients were very high-level managers, we learned. Here's what we found:
>
> Manager #1 said, "I asked my assistant to recycle it before it gets to me as it has no value for me. As a result, I haven't actually seen the report in over a year. I didn't even know you were still producing it".
>
> Manager #2 said, "Yes, I get the report, but I trash it because there's nothing in it that I need. I figured maybe one of the other guys was using it, but not me".
>
> Manager #3 said, "I get the report and put into a credenza in my office. I recycle last month's report and replace it with the new one."
>
> We asked a follow-up question, "Do you actually read it or use it?" The Manager couldn't recall doing either.
>
> Manager #4 said, "Yes, I do get the report and I use it. Once a month I look behind Tab #8 at the spreadsheet there. In it there is a cell with a number. I copy that number into a different field on another report that I submit. Oh, by the way, I know I can get the same info from the online system, but I have just gotten used to pulling if from your report."
>
> The team asked, "What do you do with the rest of the report". His answer, "Nothing".

The room fell silent, with each member staring into space. After a while, I asked, "What did you learn here?" They replied that they learned that all the effort and dedication that went into their work, along with their attempts to improve it with color charts, better layouts, etc., were ultimately useless. They were very depressed. In effect they felt that their jobs were proven to be more-or-less meaningless. Depressing indeed.

We decided to try to dig deeper to find out what had happened. Why was it that they were producing such a fine product that had no value? And why didn't they know it before now? We had to know!

After a rich discussion and a thorough root cause analysis (RCA), they determined that the report had originally been commissioned by the head of the department some seven years earlier. That person had since retired five years ago.

They further learned that a few years back, a whole new electronic system was brought online to replace the report they were creating. When asked at that time if they should stop producing it, the 'new' boss (who had also left the area since) was told, "Keep it going until we debug the new system. We'll let you know when it is no longer necessary". That call never came.

Needless to say, the team was disbanded soon after and, thankfully, they were each absorbed into other, more value-added roles. This serves as a real-life reminder that you can fall into the trap of doing the wrong work better and better.

Key Principle #4: Add Value to Your Customer

The notion of 'value' turns out to be more complex than it first appears. Our superficial understanding of it leans towards that which a customer is willing to pay for. Let's take a woman's purse as an example. The most obvious value is its form, fit and function, right? But is that all? A feedbag may serve the same purpose as a Gucci purse just as well if its sole value were derived from how much stuff it could hold.

We must look deeper to understand that value to a customer (or a patient in the healthcare setting) comes from other sources as well. So, shopping for a purse begins with its functionality, but it doesn't end there. It must have certain features at a bare minimum. Our Six Sigma teachers refer to those as elements that are 'critical to quality' or simply critical to quality (CTQs).

Beyond CTQs though, we get into a much more complex dynamics of value. We start to understand that other aspects of a product or service might matter to customers, maybe more so.

So, in the purse example, we start to look at style, color and brand name, as well. I refer to value as having at least two component properties, tangible and intangible. Also, the 'experience' of purchasing, truly an intangible, has a bearing on the customer's judgment of value. What would your fiancé think if you told her you bought her engagement ring at Costco? I mean, what difference does it really make? Ask at your own peril.

Story Time: *What Business Are We REALLY In?*

When Honda began to threaten Harley Davidson's dominance in the big motorcycle market with their elegant new Gold Wing touring motorcycle, panic ensued. Harley saw the Japanese competitor as having created a truly refined, velvety smooth, quiet piece of mechanical art. It is to this day a masterpiece of near perfect engineering.

As the story goes, Harley turned to its engineers to design a bike that would compete head-on with the Gold Wing. They developed an equally fine, quiet, and refined truly exquisite motorcycle.

When they showed the product to a focus group of loyal Harley owners, can you imagine their response? I understand that they threatened to abandon the brand altogether if Harley ever produced such a thing. They threatened to even remove their Harley tattoos. Huh? What's happening here?

To understand this phenomenon, we must dissect what value meant to their respective customers. On its surface, you would think that both companies were competing for the same buyers and that they were both in the motorized transportation business. You would be wrong. In fact, you could argue that the two companies are really in different industries and have vastly different customers.

As it turns out, Honda is in the recreation and transportation business while Harley eventually came to the realization that it is really in the image business! As the story goes, Harley quickly learned that its buyers were looking for a very specific value that had almost nothing to do with getting from point A to point B.

Harley riders overtly rejected what Honda was selling! It just wasn't an option. They bought into the mystique of rugged individualism, independence, defiance and, dare I say it, 'Made-in-America' patriotism that was reflected in their motorcycle purchase. Their bikes were really an extension of their values, not just something you sit on. Some Harley club members even ostracize fellow members showing up to club rides if they dare to show up with a Honda or any other 'brand X' product, for that matter.

As it turned out, Harley discovered that it is really selling intangible values like independence, ruggedness and individuality. They went back to the drawing board and—get this—deliberately engineered *IN* noise, vibration and harshness. That's what their customers want. And that's what Harley gives them. I guess the theory here is that not just anybody can handle a Harley.

Also, how I 'see' or eventually buy the product is also factored in. Are the purses in a jumbled pile in a dirty corner by the shoes or are they showcased carefully in isolation? Case in point: I can buy the exact same purse from either Target or from Bloomingdale's. This is when it starts to get really murky. Am I buying a purse or am I buying an experience? Hmmm.

An Example

We were vacationing in Austria when we visited the famous Swarovski Crystal headquarters there. We toured their remarkable factory and watched in amazement at how the artisans created such magnificent pieces of art.

At the end of the tour, we were led to their 'exclusive VIP showroom', where some of their signature pieces were displayed. It was more of a museum than a typical, even upscale, shop. Spread around the showroom were magnificent displays of individual round pedestals with clear glass enclosures showcasing a single product under a special light to show how the light reflected off all facets of the piece.

We fell in love with a candle holder that looked like a crystal rose. It rotated slowly under the light, sparkling like a diamond. All it took was a casual glance to the sales staff to indicate our intention to purchase a pair of these spectacular items. In a sense, it was like a celebrity silent auction. Soon they appeared from somewhere out of view with each piece in its own customized round box lined, of course, in velvet!

So here I am, years later, sharing this story with you. It is to demonstrate how an otherwise routine purchase can be transformed into a 'moment' worth sharing over and over again.

If you start to look, you will see that a great deal of advertising and merchandising is appealing directly to our *intangible* values consideration.

I don't just want to buy a shirt to cover my torso or a tie to cover the spaghetti sauce stain on my shirt. I want to project my persona, my fitness and my sense of style as well. Have you heard, "Do these jeans make my hips look big?"

As you think about your products, services, etc., can you isolate both the tangible and intangible values that *YOUR* customers want? Sometimes it is simply how they are treated during the purchase process and not even the product itself. Case in point, would you rather renew your car's registration at the American automobile association (AAA) or at the department of moter vehicles (DMV)? Either way you get the same thing, right?

In healthcare settings, we refer to this as the 'patient experience'. A great deal of effort is applied to enhancing that value every single day. So, are you selling an X-ray or are you really 'selling' confidence, trust, competence or a sense of caring?

So, to bring it back to lean, value is a core notion. A deep and CURRENT understanding of what your customers value on both levels is critically important. As an executive leader, these are the kinds of domains in which you must lead. These are the questions that you must pose to your leadership team.

Reflection Questions

- How well do we know our customers' real needs today?
- What tangible and intangibles are we marketing?
- How can our products or services be differentiated from the competition?
- Can your employees tell you what your organization's value proposition is?
- Can they articulate your 'intangible value proposition' as well? If not, why not?
- Do the mission and values statements and slogans that are posted on the wall jive with your customers' reality? (At Ford, is quality really job one?)

Other Things to Think About

Who in your company doesn't need to know what your customers value? At the Ritz-Carlton, if you ask any employee what their value proposition is, everybody will tell you the exact same thing, whether it's the housekeepers, the parking valets or the front desk staff: "We are ladies and gentlemen serving ladies and gentlemen".

The staff is empowered to make decisions that are in alignment with their interpretation of that value proposition. So, for example, if the customer asks a parking valet where she might get a good car wash in the area, the valet may, at his or her own discretion, offer to take the customer's vehicle for a car wash and have the Ritz pick up the tab.

Can you walk around your company and ask everyone, "Who are our specific customers and what do you think they value?" Will you get current, correct and complete answers? This stuff sits squarely on the shoulders of executive leaders. If you don't do it, who will? This is your sandbox, play in it.

Where Does 'Value Creation' Really Come From?

Traditional organizations are built around what we often refer to as silos or pyramids. They reflect the organization's need for command-and-control capability traceable back to post-WWII organizational structures.

Chain-of-command can be shown as a pyramid with you, the executive, at the top of your respective department. Typically, decision-making occurs within the department's own pyramid and doesn't necessarily reflect the way value is actually created for your customer. Decisions are slow and cumbersome and, all too often, wrong. They are utterly detached from what we now like to refer to as *the situation on the ground.*

In Figure 7.2a, you are atop your department or your company. Under you are one or more value streams that you are ultimately responsible for.

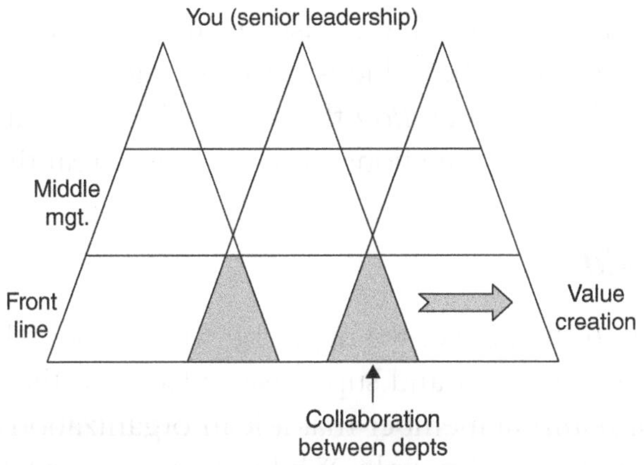

Figure 7.2a

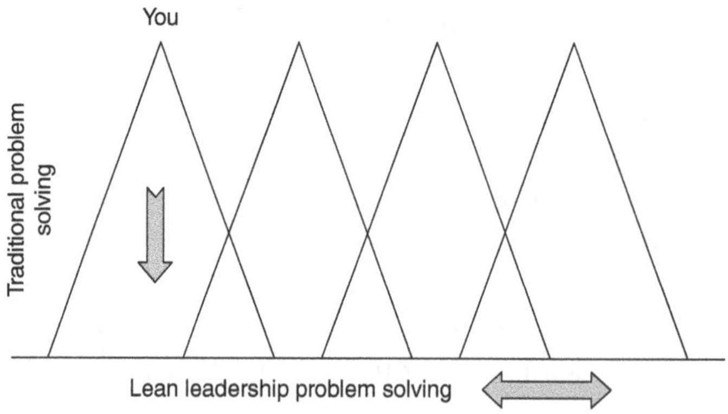

Figure 7.2b

You will commonly interact with your peers on a regular, if infrequent, basis, maybe weekly or monthly. Typically, decision-making and control flow vertically, usually downward.

At the bottom of your department are those who are actually creating the value for your customers, like a nurse giving a patient an injection. As a product moves through your organization, the workers must collaborate horizontally as the work flows from pyramid to pyramid (e.g., from design to engineering, to sales, to manufacturing, to shipping, etc.). Think relay race.

If the workers must rely on the department's chain-of-command to resolve issues, make decisions, solve problems, etc., it slows down value creation and creates possible missed opportunities (Figure 7.2b). The workers must wait for answers, decisions, problem resolution, etc., coming from on high via the relatively infrequent contact between department heads, etc., to take place. Typically, organizations like this are slow, bureaucratic and burdensome.

In a lean enterprise, those same decisions, answers, etc., often occur at the bottom, close to where the value is actually being created. Workers have the freedom, indeed the *expectation* that they will collaborate continuously with their peers in adjacent functions in more-or-less real time.

The Missing Middle

As we think through the above, we might be wondering, what about those middle layers of management and supervision? How do they fit in? *This is a super important point!* Remember that a lean organization needs fewer but more highly empowered people. While this is a potentially huge cost savings, it is not to be taken lightly. Cost savings, again, are not the point!

Creating an agile, customer-centered, competitive organization full of highly motivated and empowered people is!

Frequently, organizations adopting lean overlook this critically important aspect of their transformation into a flatter, more empowered one. It is common for executives like you to create the vision and get excited about the future you can now imagine. But many execs from their lofty perches on mahogany row will overlook the severe consequences of NOT planning for these crucially important layers. They can be strong advocates for you, or they could be insulating the front line from your messaging. Ignore this group at your own peril.

With your coach, I recommend a clear and thorough plan be created with serious input from those who are now feeling that they are at risk and that includes how to address this issue. Take great care to think it through area by area, person by person, name by name.

The basic strategy here is to

- Guarantee equivalent work and pay!
- Fully engage with these managers and supervisors and seek their input and perspective. Act on them when you can. **NOTE**: You will have to be very discerning here to embrace legitimate ideas and not succumb to underlying delay and diversion tactics disguised as serious issues.
- Train these layers of supervision *more deeply than anyone else* to become coaches in the new order.
- Allow for unexpected departures; sometimes even those you most wanted to keep. Remember that change can evoke fear and could prompt others to find less turmoil and stress elsewhere.
- Grandfather individuals in current roles as appropriate. Example, if you have an existing manager who is near retirement age, you may want to allow that person to stay on as a consultant and plan on eliminating that position when it becomes vacant.

These next drawings can help you frame the evolution necessary to get from your current leadership comfort zone into a new paradigm that allows for maximum self-management and organic problem-solving at the lowest possible level in the organization. Take a minute to digest them as a sequential set. The idea here is that you have a mental model of how you can begin to transition from a leader dependent model to a *leader as coach* model.

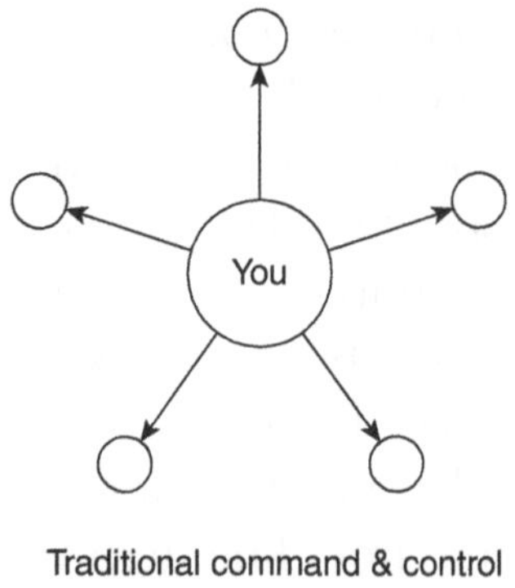

Figure 7.3a

Crucial point: You can and should recreate these images for your team. You want them to see *you*, not a consultant or staffer, as their teacher and coach. You are building your legacy.

1. Here in Figure 7.3a, we see a typical 'command and control' communication pattern. You are at the center and serve as the 'dispatcher' of information, decisions, answers, problem-solving, etc. Note that the arrows indicate a one-way direction from you to the team in orbit around you. Think of a sergeant giving orders to the troops.
2. In this slightly evolved model (Figure 7.3b), you are still in its center but with a two-way dialogue between you and those within your 'control'.

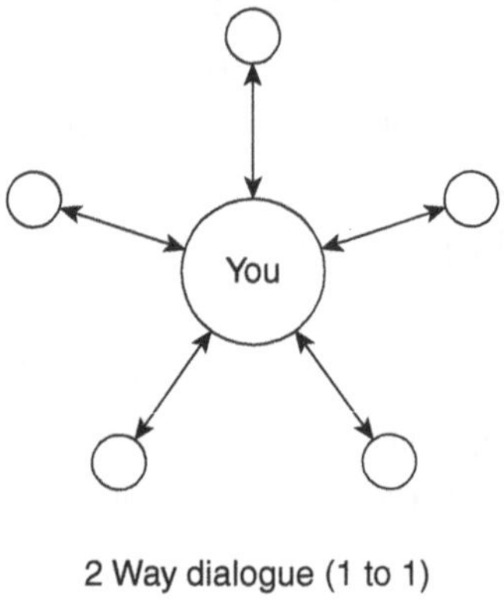

Figure 7.3b

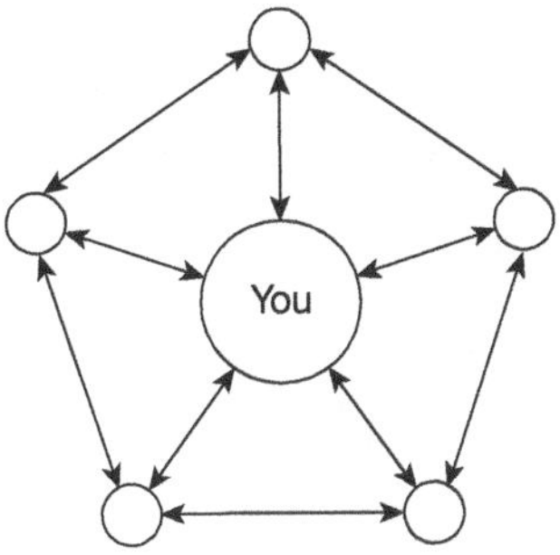

Team dialogue – Staff meeting

Figure 7.3c

This implies that you are both informing and soliciting input from the team. Think football quarterback in a huddle.

3. Still further evolved, in Figure 7.3c, you can see that communication, decision-making and problem-solving involve the team connecting with one another, but still revolves around you as the center pole of the tent. Think team meetings.
4. As we evolve still further, as in Figure 7.3d, you are now a critical partner in the team, but no longer the center point. You may still serve as the facilitator or linchpin but no longer the primary decision maker. The team is beginning to think and act more and more independently. They are becoming a coherent 'leaderless' team. Think coach.

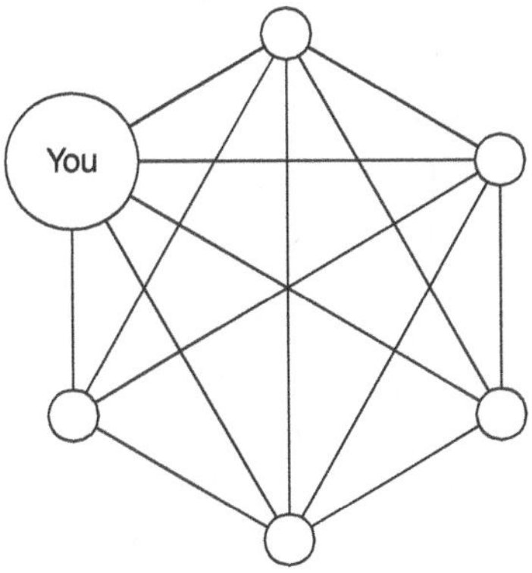

'Facilitator' model

Figure 7.3d

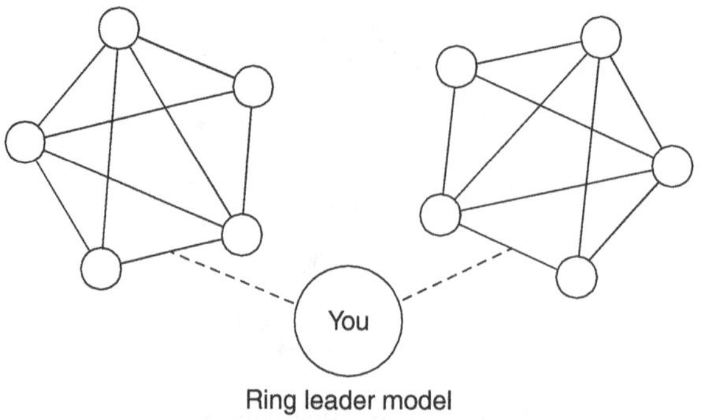

Figure 7.3e

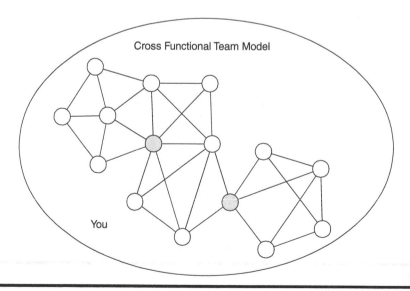

5. In Figure 7.3e, you are now evolving and, more importantly, your team has evolved to a point where they now rely on each other, pulling you in as necessary to perform tasks that may be beyond their scope (e.g., collaborating externally with other departments or even the entire organization). You are now an ad hoc 'resource' to the team, but it functions normally with little if any direct input from you. Think circus ringleader.
6. Figure 7.3f represents the final stage of your lean leadership evolution and takes you to a level where semi-autonomous, cross-functional teams are now connected to each other by means of overlapping,

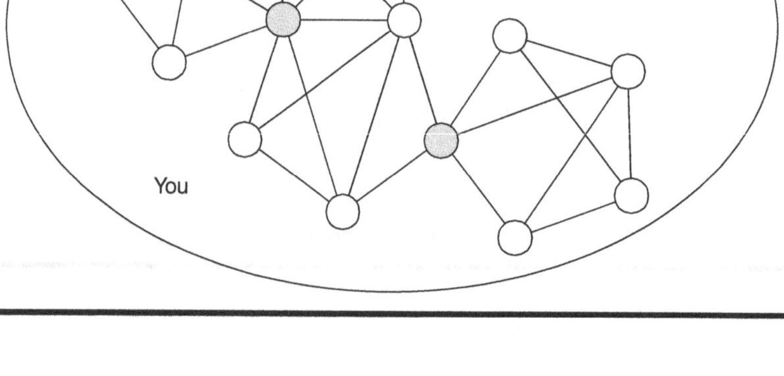

Figure 7.3f

linchpin roles and responsibilities. This is a highly fluid and adaptable configuration where teams are empowered around the organizational mission vs. individual department goals.

Here is an example: Marketing staff contributing actively and equally in manufacturing meetings. Shared governance is now the norm. These teams even do their own recruiting and make hiring decisions independently. You now coach and develop almost exclusively and provide little, if any, day-to-day direction. Think orchestra conductor.

Key Principle #5: Visual Management (VM)

When you walk to your office from the parking lot, how do you know if your business is healthy or not? Are you winning or losing, right now, at this very moment? Do you have to rely on meetings or reports to figure it out?

This is one of many reasons that the lean approach relies heavily on visual management to know exactly what is going on minute-to-minute. We use charts and graphs for this purpose, but are the 'stories' being told by those charts really useful? Nice to know? Critical? A waste of time and paper? Are your indicators leading or lagging? A weather report is a lagging indicator; a weather forecast is a leading indicator!

Learning from Surfers

Growing up at the beach in Southern California, I was destined to become a surfer. I remember being coached by other, more experienced surfers to look over my shoulder constantly. Why? You need to be able to 'read' the waves that are approaching (leading indicator).

When you see the perfect size and shape coming, you want to begin to paddle BEFORE it gets to you and then allow the energy of the wave to carry you. Timing is everything in surfing. You can't wait until the wave gets to you to start paddling. Or, as was my own tendency, start too late and have the perfect wave slide beneath me. A common rookie mistake. We used to yell at other surfers from the pier overhead, too. We'd see the perfect wave from that vantage point better than they could from being in the water. "Go, go, go!" we would shout.

As your organization's top leader, you must be able to see the 'waves' coming at you in the market you are in with equal clarity.

Some Questions

- Are you confident in your ability to see what's coming?
- Have you experienced missed waves of opportunity or risk that you should have been able to prepare for?
- Do you take advantage of different perspectives and sources to help you see what's coming?
- Can your staff see what you can't?

This is the essence of the visual management system lean will create for you. Simple, direct, instantaneous communication. As stated before, the goal is to create visuals that are easily understood from five feet away in five seconds or less; it is also known as the 5 × 5 rule.

We are used to visual management. It's everywhere: street signs, signals, symbols, etc. Lean takes visual management into the workplace so that we are all be able to see at a glance what's working and what's not. Every person is a company associate with a stake in its success.

One Japanese derivative of visual management heard frequently in lean circles is the Andon (translates simply to light). See Chapter 4, "Lean Speak". Typically, it is a board with numbers corresponding to areas in a plant and workflow condition lights.

As you would expect, a green, white or no light corresponding to a given area means everything is within expected limits. A yellow or red light means that something abnormal is going on and that attention is required.

Sometimes these lights are supplemented by sounds or even specific melodies that inform the team in the event you don't happen to be looking up at the Andon board. Visual management takes on many other forms as well. Sometimes simple colored cards will be used to convey similar situations. The key is that you should be able to determine the health of your enterprise without relying on reports or meetings. Think of this as a system that shows the 'vital signs' of your enterprise continuously.

Let's consider your car's dashboard for a minute. On it there is critical information available to you at all times. You want to know your speed, your fuel level and maybe even your location on a GPS. So, gauges like the speedometer, fuel level, etc., are always displayed in front of you. But, and this is important, you don't need or want to see information that is only relevant ***IF*** something abnormal is going on.

Frankly, I don't care what my oil pressure is at any given moment. I just want to trust that a warning light will come on if it isn't within the normal

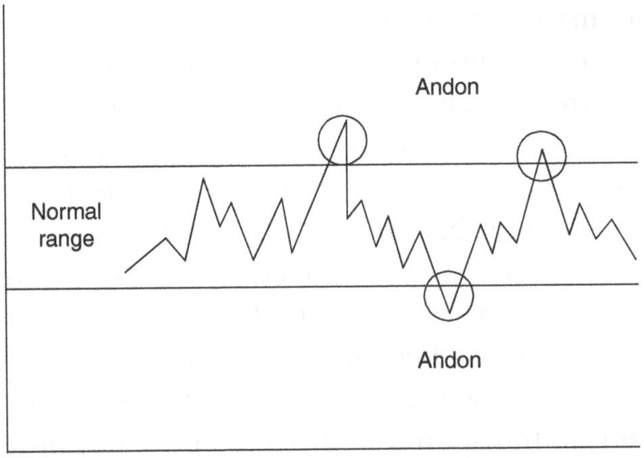

Figure 7.4

range. Ditto for tire pressure and all the other warnings that only illuminate in abnormal conditions. In Figure 7.4, you can see that the warning or Andon signal would illuminate at the points shown, but not in the normal operating range or quality parameters.

We tend to use the term 'dashboard' in business pretty loosely. When you think about it, it's likely that yours contains information that doesn't demand your attention. Why look at data that are within normal limits? Your focus must be on those things that are NOT normal, and your communications and visual management systems should screen out everything else.

Random Thought

What is the most important part of a car? Yes, there *IS* a right answer! It is simply the part of the car that doesn't work! So, if you have a flat, that tire becomes the most important part of your car at that moment. The same logic applies to your business's visual management system. It needs to constantly alert you to what is broken or is about to break. Does yours?

Key Principle #6: Make Problems Visible

Pay close attention here. This is a big deal.

Sadly, we have created a work culture within which it is commonplace to hide problems. It is regrettable that our employees have learned, often the hard way, to bury issues, deny responsibility for mistakes and often devolve into blaming others and finger pointing. Think Congress.

This has led to management in general, and you the executive, being blind to the real issues confronting your operations. The consequences of this type of culture can have a devastating, if not fatal, effect on your business. No, it is not too much of a leap of faith to conclude that it could ultimately lead to the failure of your enterprise. This is a big deal!

Sugar-coating issues can be a milder form of the same problem but can lead to distractions and rework as you chase down the wrong problems or go down endless rabbit holes trying to find the real problem let alone its root cause. Painting over rust becomes the norm.

The antidote to the above is to create, or in some cases recreate, a culture of blame-free transparency. Toyota, under the broader heading of 'respect for people', actually thanks and REWARDS team members for surfacing problems. They are shown great respect and in a very conspicuous fashion for candidly sharing even their own mistakes! Their approach can be summarized by Ohno's quote that, "The absence of a problem, is a problem".

Creating a 'Problems First' Mentality

Story Time: *Fail Faster Than Your Competition*

Failure forums: This involves having meetings, etc., where the 'price of admission' to the meeting is a relevant problem. The origins of this came from an astute observation coming from top Toyota executives upon visiting US operations. During these meetings, it was noticed that there was a predictable and continuing trend to showcase all the great things that were going on within a specific area of operation being visited, giving the false impression that everything was hunky-dory.

The effect of this was to have meetings that were completely consumed by all the positive things that were going on, leaving little if any time for the visiting executives to (a) understand the problems that were occurring and (b) to learn about opportunities to remove barriers or obstacles to progress.

Instituting this policy changed the corporate culture, and it became the norm that meetings with these executives *started* with the problems facing the business areas, with the presumption that many great things were going on, but limited time required a critical focus. Those same visitors would ask us to let our staffs come to the meetings so that the information being shared was coming directly from those most directly affected by it at the front line.

This one change shifted the focus to solving real problems utterly and completely. It was very weird at first but, once we accepted that the visiting execs were sincere in their desire to help and not place blame, we looked forward to those meetings. Naturally, it also resulted in subordinate leaders prepping for those meetings by shopping around for problems prior to the visiting executive's arrival. Nobody wanted to say that they DIDN'T have any problems after that. What a transformation that simple change made!

While at first this process may require folks to stick their necks out and display some courage, it can also be the tipping point in changing the culture. This seemingly simple change in leadership approach can cause a shift to making problems visible, dramatically increasing trust in leadership and promoting efficiency in solving the right problem the first time. It also provided a perfect opportunity to coach and develop our people.

A common axiom that you will hear within the lean culture is that there are *Good people in a bad process*. You will also hear the phrase, *Nobody comes to work to deliberately do a bad job*. Whether or not these quotes are literally true is subject to some speculation, but the notion is indicative of fostering and rewarding a blame-free culture.

Story Time: *First Learn the Rules; Then Break Them*

When I worked in the headquarters of a very prominent aerospace company, I had a rather unique experience from the pre-lean period of my career (otherwise known as the dark ages). I was an internal HR manager. I was assigned to a key leader, Tom, as his HR liaison. We became great friends, and he even became the best man at my wedding!

Nevertheless, I recall vividly an event that occurred when we were assembling for a routine weekly management team meeting. I sat next to Tom on his right. As the team gathered around a gigantic conference table, even before the meeting started, Tom reached across the large table to one of his leaders, George. As he extended his hand across the table to shake George's hand, he said, "Congratulations, I just heard the news of your colossal failure on your last project! It cost us millions!" It wreaked of sarcasm!

I was mortified, as was every other leader present. I was kicking Tom under the table as he held George's hand for an awkwardly long time, both stretched across the table. I tried to get him to stop! "What the hell are you thinking? What's gotten into you?" I said to him in a very emphatic whisper, hoping no one else would hear me.

He simply smiled at me and continued to hold George's hand across the table. The other leaders were now obviously nervous. You can imagine what George was thinking.

Eventually he let go and they both sat down. He then said, "Thank you, George! You are the only one here who had the guts to try something different. You took me at my word that I wanted to break our paradigms and try new things. While your specific project failed, I am immensely proud of you. I know that you will share your learnings from it so we can all benefit. I consider it an investment in learning".

He then went on to say as he scanned the other faces around the table, "We can all learn from George! He is a true and courageous leader. We just can't rest on our laurels and not challenge ourselves continuously. We are really in a laboratory environment here. We need to blow stuff up if we're ever gonna get better! We ARE the lunatic fringe. Let's act like it!"

Imagine my relief. It gave me chills to see real leadership in action. He knew the 'rules' but also when to break them. To this day, I am inspired by his faith in his leadership team and his willingness to embrace failure as the inevitable consequence of trying and learning. From that day forth, the other leaders began to wade into risks that they had avoided completely before that fateful meeting. That was Tom's legacy. What will yours be?

My Recommendations

Work with your leadership team to understand how pervasive this culture may be in your company. Once you establish if there are indeed issues of concern, communicate to all hands your concern about those things and your intent to change them with their help and guidance. You must ensure that ALL your leaders, managers and supervisors at all levels are held accountable to perpetuate a transparent culture.

Anything less will lead to your direction and ambition being diluted, 'translated', ignored or systematically undermined. Stay open to the fact that you may, regrettably, have to separate these leaders from your company who do not align themselves with this culture shift. Anything less will perpetuate cynicism and make your staff go deeper underground and bury problems. This is your opportunity to truly lead. Use your coach and HR resources carefully here. Beware, this could be thin ice!

Another recommendation that I frequently make to my clients is to perpetuate the idea of 'Failure Forums'. As the stated before, the price of admission to these meetings is that you must be ready to present a 'failure' with a bias toward what you learned from it and how others might benefit from your experiences. This goes a long way toward reinforcing a culture of experimentation, risk taking and breakthrough, out-of-the-box thinking.

You may have adopted the often-repeated expression, "Don't bring me problems; bring me solutions!" While on its surface, this seems reasonable enough. But what happens after you say that? What if there are real problems for which a solution is not yet known? Should we just ignore them? Are we asking our team to just suck it up if they don't have the time, knowledge or courage to come forward with a 'solution' that might risk ridicule if it's not optimal? Over time, they will just keep problems to themselves. What are the consequences of that?

In my opinion, Toyota probably 'fails' more than most big corporations. When you think about it, failure by itself is not a differentiator. What IS a differentiator is what happens AFTER a failure. Toyota's rich learning routines serve as a safety net by ensuring that rigorous postmortem processes occur consistently. Case in point: The failure of the Toyota Echo led to the breakthrough in Scion. The failure of the Cressida led to Lexus. The failure of the T100 truck led to the Tundra. There's a pattern here. Failure can be the rocket fuel of introspection and innovation; the crucible from which breakthroughs are spawned. Some use the acronym, F.A.I.L. which equals *First Attempt in Learning.*

Reflection Questions

- Would anyone entering your work areas know in an instant how things are going?
- How might you enhance your visual management system to highlight problems?
- Do you and all leaders in your organization actively encourage your employees to candidly share problems, errors and other mistakes without fear?
- Are you failing enough to stimulate reflection and learning?
- Are you obsessed with playing it safe?

Key Principle #7: Maintain a Long-Term Perspective

Many companies that I have worked with have an obsession with short-term results. Their motives are legitimate enough but there may be severe downside risks. In the car biz, they tend to measure their sales results in ten-day cycles. This can put long-term goals in jeopardy. Some scenarios that exacerbate this short-term focus are: prepping for board meetings, meeting shareholder expectations, quick wins in market share and the general sense of immediate gratification and inertia.

Sometimes we telegraph this phenomenon by big sales and product promotions. *Act Now* is the mantra that is a dead giveaway that there's a level of urgency reflecting our short-term needs. In the auto industry, there will be the inevitable year-end sales push to sell every unit possible before December 31. Deep discounts are made to achieve those objectives. But what happens in January? Typically, sales slump markedly as a natural consequence of pulling sales forward into the prior year. Now what?

Some companies also keep a close eye on what are termed *True North* goals. These are very stable goals that are directional in nature, hence the term. They tend to be very lofty and might even be perceived as unachievable. One such true north goal that I particularly liked was, *To be a responsible steward of the earth.* Lofty indeed. Sure, many companies will have them. Having true north goals is not by itself a differentiator. What does differentiate is the degree to which a company maintains a steady focus on them year in and year out.

It is up to you as an executive to balance the short-term objectives with those long-term ambitions. So, yes, we want to sell a lot in the current month. But we also want to ensure that we have products that will always meet the customers' needs over the long haul. An obsession with monthly sales would not have produced the Prius for example. Nobody ever said to Toyota, "Build me a gas/electric hybrid vehicle and I'll buy it". It came under the broad umbrella, True North Hoshin of being "better stewards of planet Earth".

The term 'vision' comes to mind as we seek to keep at least one eye looking out over the horizon. Wayne Gretzky, aka *The Great One*, was famously asked how he became known as the greatest hockey player in history. His response was, "I skate to where the puck is going to be, not to where it has been." Your vision and long-term perspective should embrace that notion. Where will your company (and your competitors) be ten years from now?

Reflection Questions

- What are your long-term ambitions over the next five to ten years? Your ten-year plan?
- How often do you review them?
- Are there strategies in place to achieve them?
- Does everybody in the company understand them? If not, why not?
- Are they inspiring to your employees?

Key Principle #8: Simplicity

This is one of my favorite topics. As we addressed earlier, we claim we prefer simplicity and yet we rarely miss a chance to make things more complicated. Complication is one of those things that tends to happen gradually over a period of time. A dominant theme of complexity is found in its host, bureaucracy. Over time, we add layer upon layer of addendums, deviations, exceptions, rules, policies, etc., etc., etc.

A Hypothetical …

Imagine for a moment that you are decorating a Christmas tree from many boxes of treasured ornaments. Each one represents a fond memory of a time and place or a loved one who contributed it to your collection.

You decorate using the unwritten rule that every ornament must be hung on every tree every year. The process requires that you carefully unwrap each one and reflect on it. It might sound something like this, "Awww, we got this Surfing Santa ornament from my Aunt Mary. She picked it up for us when she was visiting Maui. I miss Aunt Mary, don't you? She was such a gem …". After you have recounted the same story that you have repeated year after year, you eventually hang it in just the right spot on just the right bough.

You repeat this process with every ornament until all the boxes are empty and every single one is now on the tree. When you stand back to admire your beautiful Christmas tree, you suddenly realize you can barely see the tree anymore. There are so many ornaments, you wonder if the tree will fall over under the weight.

This is similar to organizational complexity. Over the years, we have added so much weight on ourselves that we can barely maneuver. Every legacy project, like the ornaments, has its own story. Each is beautiful in its own right and made perfect sense when it was added but how much can the organization stand before it takes its toll on your company?

You start to notice that everything seems slower now than it used to be. Everybody's pet project is sacred. Nobody wants to take anything away. We don't really know how to sunset work very well.

I had an executive client, Patti, suffering from this malady in her department. She had a non-exempt team member, Carol, who was in charge of the cataloguing and storage of all their policies. We went to visit her. Carol sat in a room that looked like a giant law library. It was spotless. She oversaw all the corporate policies, which sat in neat rows of big three ring binders filling shelves from end to end. An entire room was dedicated to them. She had even developed a system for cataloguing them.

I asked her how she knew when and how to eliminate obsolete policies. She looked at me seriously and said, "We've never done that before. At least not in the ten years that I've been doing this". I followed up with, "Well, if you had to eliminate some, how would you go about it?" She stumbled with the question. "To be honest, I don't even know how we would do it", she said glancing over to see Patti's reaction.

I asked her how the policies were used. She said sometimes she will get a call to clarify a policy and then she starts to find that policy in her system. Then, after she locates it, she'll go to the originator of the policy, if that person even exists anymore, and ask for the clarification. Of course, I had to ask, "What if the originator is no longer around? Then what?"

She said, "Oh that happens all the time. I then go to the department that the originator came from and ask around if anybody there knows anything about the policy. Usually, they don't though". "Then what?", I asked. "Well", she said, "I go back to the person who requested the clarification and ask how urgent the need was. If they say it's no big deal, I just file the request away for some further research when I get the time. Which is never", she added.

I asked her, "What do you do if the request really is urgent?" "Well, then I request to work overtime. Usually, I can eventually find what I'm looking for, but there's never enough time during my regular hours".

I have to say that Carol was one of the most determined workers I have ever met. But I had images of her on a treadmill in my head. I kept wondering where this insanity would eventually end. I kept that thought to myself, but I did ask her, "In your cataloguing system, can you sort them by the date that they were created or last revised?" She said, "Not really. They are sorted by type, originating department and by which other policies might also be relevant. You know, cross-referencing them".

I thanked her and complimented her on her diligence and attention to detail. Patti asked me what I thought as we made our way back to her office. "Any advice?" she asked. "Three things", I said. Here's what I told her:

1. If you had a system of dates for each, you could then sort them by the oldest to newest and begin to evaluate how relevant they might be. It would be great if you could discard half of them. But if you can't, maybe you could establish an age range for 'obsolete' policies and store them away in some archive.
2. Another thought I had was to establish an expiration date on every policy, like a carton of milk, and then systematically review each one when they became due for revision.
3. Remind your other execs that policies are no more than routine answers to routine questions. They are not good for everything new that happens and may never happen again. They are terrible at handling the singular and the exceptional situations. Creating policies sounds like it's just a knee-jerk reaction when people don't know how to handle new issues, so creating policies has become a habit and it's institutionalized now. You have paved the cow path, so to speak.

As we sat down back at Patti's desk, I drew the sketches that follow.

On Baseball and Bureaucracy

I glanced around her office and noticed several baseball artifacts. "Do you like baseball?" I asked. She said, "I'm a big Dodgers fan, can't you tell? Why?" I drew a picture of a baseball diamond. "Look familiar?" I asked. "Yes, of course", she nodded wondering where this was all going.

So in Figure 7.5a, we have a standard baseball diamond with the normal nine players on the field. Imagine that this is the bottom of the

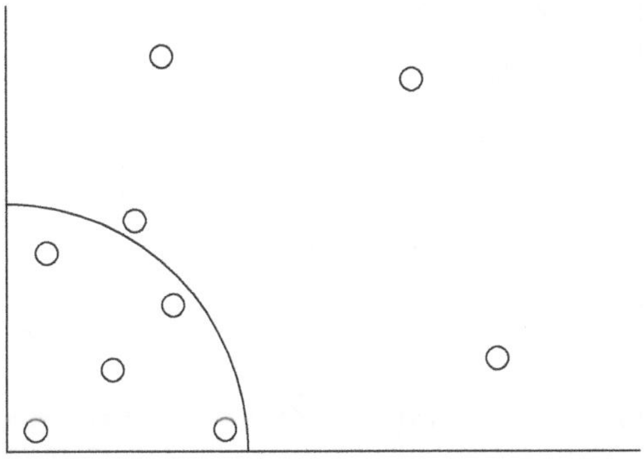

Figure 7.5a

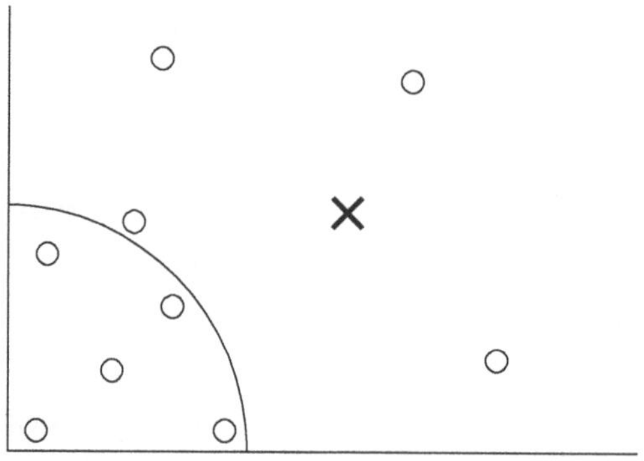

Figure 7.5b

ninth inning of the seventh game in the World Series and the score is tied. Bases loaded.

In Figure 7.5b, the Dodgers are in the field. The opposing team's batter just hit the ball right here at the 'x'.

I said to Patti, "The Center Fielder watches the ball land". He figures that the ball is in right field and watches for the right fielder to go after it. Meanwhile, the right fielder thinks the ball is in center field and so, he watches the center fielder, expecting him to catch it.

Throughout this confusion, the first and second basemen are watching them both, wondering who the hell is going to go after the damn ball! Meanwhile, the opposing team scores. End of game. The Dodgers just lost the World Series due to an unforced error.

What happened?

Figure 7.5c: During the postseason, the Dodgers decided that the actual problem that caused them to lose was that there was no 'Right

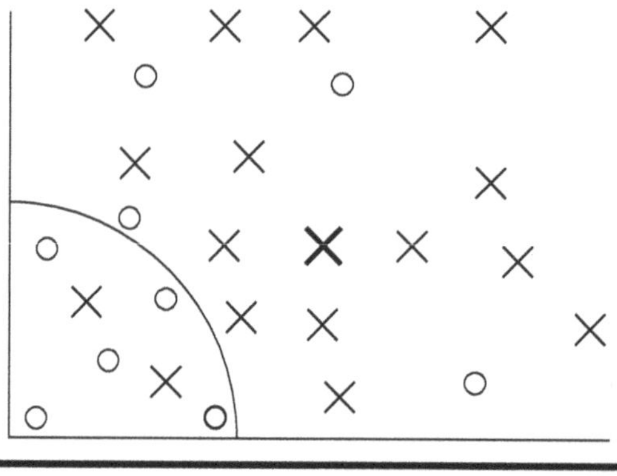

Figure 7.5c

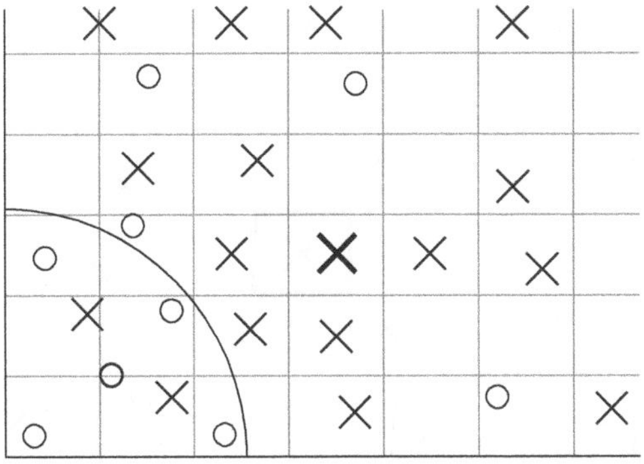

Figure 7.5d

Center Fielder' who could have caught the ball. So, the following season, they created one. And it worked. In fact, it worked so well, that they decided to add a 'Left Center Fielder', too. And then, an 'Inner Diamond Fielder', and then a 'Right Side Shortstop' to prevent the First and Second Basemen from also missing a ball due to role confusion. We're really onto something now, right?

Eventually, as shown in Figure 7.5d, there were now 50 players on the field. To prevent confusion, they decided to re-stripe the field so that everybody now has their own box to stand in. The rules must be changed, too. After all, we can't have players going outside their boxes, right? In fact, you build a wall around each box to prevent players from doing so.

I asked Patti a question, "Did you ever wonder why there are no stripes dividing the outfield into three parts? It's because there is an expectation that every player places a priority on the ball, not on their formal title as shown on their baseball cards. They are taught to go for the ball and to communicate with one another, right? It is not only OK for the right fielder to venture into center field, but it is also expected! And it is rewarded!"

"OK, enough already. I'm sure you get the point by now," I told her. "This is what has happened to your company over the years. Instead of going back to the original problem, which was the players not communicating with each other by calling the ball or, God forbid, BOTH going for the ball, you decided it was an 'organizational gap' that needed to be closed by hiring specialists who were only expected to stay in their respective boxes. You taught them to wait until the ball drops into their chimney, and if it does, just throw

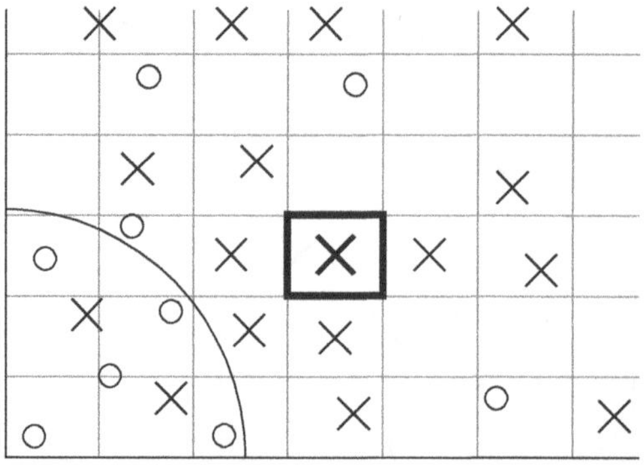

Figure 7.5e

it out. Somebody else will deal with it. They can't see the other players. They don't even know if they're winning or losing. And it's no fun playing anymore".

"To further reinforce the need for organization", I explained, "you reinforced the walls of policies, procedures, rules, chain-of-command structures, signature authority, purchasing rules, org charts, training and job descriptions that served to prevent collaboration or communication between boxes and stifled any sense of personal accountability or empowerment (Figure 7.5e). All in the name of 'managing the organization'. Who wants chaos, right? What we have now is a full-blown bureaucracy! It wasn't intentional, it just happened, and nobody even noticed it. It became your corporate culture by default, not by design."

Patti stared numbly at me. After an especially long and silent pause, she eventually spoke, "Yikes, what can we do about that now?" My advice to her was to share this metaphor with her leadership team and ask them if this is the way they really want the place to be. If not, then start to dismantle the walls, knock down barriers and remove obstacles.

Loosen up the rules. Push decision-making down lower in the organization. Encourage the players to knock down the walls between adjacent positions and to start to promote a game-within-a-game of sorts. Train your teams in problem-solving and critical thinking. Cross-train like crazy! Give them a sense of ownership any way you can. Reward players who step out of their normal roles. That will encourage others to follow.

I also recommended that they resist the temptation to continuously and habitually add new players. Over time, I told her, you will start to see your organization becoming more agile, more flexible, more profitable and, yes, more fun! You will see reduced turnover and lower recruiting costs. Your employee opinion scores will improve steadily. Discretionary effort will soar!

Sure, it will take time, but five years from now, you will be amazed at the transformation. Oh, and by the way, your competitors will be quaking in their shoes. But make no mistake about it, it won't fix itself! You must fix it. This is what leaders are supposed to do.

Random Thought

What would happen to a bonsai tree if you only watered it? Even if you did it correctly? If you don't trim it and shape it and clip off the branches that don't fit your image of it, you would eventually have just a *bush-in-a-bowl*, right? Your culture is like that. It requires daily tending to train it to look like what you want. This is what a daily management system is designed to do.

Even bonsai plants are not alike. There are many species like cedars, pines, etc. Even with proper pruning, you can't change their basic DNA. This is true of company cultures, as well. An aerospace company culture is not going to be the same as a post office culture. A church culture is not going to be like Google's culture. You have to work with what you have, but you can make any culture better by continuous care and feeding. Just don't leave it to chance or you will end up like Patti's company.

Chapter 8

How Will Lean Leadership Affect Me Personally?

Your role as leader will change. Your definition of yourself will change. Your legacy will change. One can't escape the comparison of the metamorphosis from caterpillar to butterfly. You will come to understand that, once you have made this transition completely, there is no going back. The good news is that you won't want to. I doubt that butterflies yearn to be caterpillars again. Nevertheless, for most of us, it is an irreversible process. Maybe the good old days weren't so good, after all.

Stop here and ask yourself this question: "What do I want my legacy to be?" Simple question but not always easy to answer. We don't tend to think too much about that sort of thing. Most of us focus on the present, getting the job done, completing projects, fighting fires and tending to the whack-a-mole crisis du jour. We don't stop often to think about what we are doing to prepare the next generation of leaders and problem solvers, let alone how we might be remembered in the future. How do you make the people around you feel? This is how they will remember you.

A Word about Personality

This can be tricky. I'm not going to go into a deep discussion of Myers-Briggs–type personality assessments here. But we must be honest about ourselves, and I owe it to you to be frank about this. Many highly successful executives rose in the ranks having built a reputation for getting things done. We are taught to be action oriented and produce results. We take no prisoners!

We have taken on the role of leader as one who is always in charge. Command-and-control are our go-to styles and we are expected to be fixated on short-term goals. After all, this is what many companies want in an executive and they recruit for those traits and expect proof that you can produce those results.

Often, this is an attribute that the shareholders and, by extension, the board of directors are looking for as well. It is often about maximizing return. Rarely will they ask about your culture, except to the extent that it impacts the bottom line. An example here might be turnover. While it may be an important barometer of your culture, often the main concern here is not why folks are leaving but what is the effect of a revolving door on P&L.

While there are many other traits that combine to make execs successful, the above is a common one in Western cultures today. Those who don't seem to possess those same traits may be seen as weak leaders. Ironically, many of these stereotypical leaders really don't like to be this way and aren't naturally wired this way but have learned that behaving as a mega boss is what is expected. They had to adapt. Many have told me privately that they feel that they must act in these 'strong and decisive' ways even though it doesn't feel natural to them.

Here's the rub. Perfecting a lean leader model requires a personal evolution from the above to a coaching and, yes, more nurturing style. If you are to be successful as a lean leader, you must be willing to shed the command-and-control skin that you have been so handsomely compensated for throughout your career. Gulp.

As you would expect, leaders who naturally adopt lean leadership behaviors tend to have a more open, humble style and therefore tend to adopt lean leadership more easily and will become vastly more successful as a result. Sadly, these same leaders are often overlooked as C-suite leaders.

Does this mean that a leader with a traditional command-and-control bias cannot be successful lean leaders? No, it doesn't. It does mean that it may require some unlearning, though. There are one or two other options to consider. Either adopt new and uncomfortable styles or, dare I say it, delegate this to another leader in your midst who may possess these traits already.

Of course, you will still be the ultimate leader, but it may be that there are others who can be more successful at it. I have seen both of these approaches work. Here are just two examples.

Two Different Approaches to Lean Leadership Transformation

1. I coached the CEO of a privately held medium-size software company who desperately wanted to have his organization transition to lean. His motives were pure, and he knew that the benefits to his company were substantial in every way. But every time a front-line team made a presentation from an improvement (kaizen) project, for example, he would shake his head uncontrollably.

   He would try to catch himself, but he couldn't accept allowing work to proceed that he absolutely KNEW would fail, even if the consequences of failure were minimal or inconsequential. I would signal to him from the back of the room to stop sending negative signals and allow his teams the opportunity to learn and grow, but he just couldn't stop himself.

   After many attempts at coaching him, we finally concluded that he was not going to be a leader who would make it happen. Reluctantly, he chose his next in command to take over the transformation and report progress back to him. He realized that he was the major obstacle to his own ambition and, for the benefit of the whole, took himself out of the primary leader role.

   Ultimately, it worked out well and the organization made gigantic strides after he took himself off the field, so to speak. As is often the case, he also learned that the lean projects that he had expected to fail were actually wildly successful! Humility happened.
2. I was coaching the president of a large, public healthcare system. He too struggled mightily with the very concept of, as he put it, "turning over the asylum to the inmates". After many hours together, he concluded that this was not an abdication of his responsibilities but rather a chance to tap into an exceptionally large and untapped pool of creativity and innovation that the lean methodology could unleash.

   He decided he would instead become a 'conspicuous student'. He communicated very openly to his large team that he had indeed decided that, if this thing was ever going to be successful, he needed to learn like everybody else. He attended all training, meetings and projects not as the boss but as a student, as a team member. As a result, he also became a major role model in the process.

   The results were remarkable. His willingness to humble himself was a sign of strength, and his credibility soared as a result. Eventually, he said publicly that undergoing this metamorphosis was the most freeing experience of his life. He no longer had to be the decider-in-chief and the all-knowing parent of his 5,000 people. It was fun to watch. That was his legacy.

As for me personally, I eventually came to the shocking reality that I had been focused on the wrong things most of my working life. I made a conscious decision, a choice really, that I wanted to be remembered not for how many projects I completed or my impact on the bottom line but rather for how many lives I had impacted. Think about this: is it your resume that you want to be read at your funeral? Is that what you want those who grieve your passing to recall about you?

Not me. I want to be remembered as a person who helped others grow and become successful. For me, that would be a tribute and a legacy worth leaving! So, how will you be remembered if you died today?

Another Way to Think about This

This is the transition from player to coach, really. It is time to get off the field and onto the sidelines. Great coaches in sports have eternal legacies that even surpass their own records on the field of play. Think Phil Jackson. Not many people can tell you much about his accomplishments as a prominent NBA player. But everybody knows that, as a coach, he is a legend.

Lean leadership paves the way for you to live a life of growing others, of building a lasting legacy. But remember, the leader transition from boss to coach is for most people, a one-way trip.

Consider this: Imagine that your three-year-old asks innocently "Mommy, how do you spell 'cat'?" How would you answer? I imagine you would say something like, "Why don't you get your blocks and let's sound it out". You would help your little girl sound out every letter, one at a time, right? Then you would help her put the sounds together, C – A – T!

Now let's jump ahead ten years. Same kid, now 13, asks the same question. "Mommy, how do you spell 'cat'?" You stare in disbelief and ask yourself, "Where have I gone wrong?" At some point, you will probably say something like, "Why are you asking me"? or "Go look it up!" Or "What have you tried?" Or other similar responses. What's different?

At some level, we realize that we have had implicit expectations that our kids will become more and more self-sufficient and independent. We feel like we've failed if our kids don't become fully functional, responsible adults.

You EXPECTED your kids to grow and mature and when they didn't, you were worried about them.

You expected that, when they first used crayons to make pictures in kindergarten, they might not look exactly like the real world. You wouldn't correct your kid's first attempts at drawing by saying, "Well, sweetie, you drew the sky purple. That's wrong. Go back and do it again correctly this time. Redo the sky in blue!" At least I hope you wouldn't. You saw it as a first attempt that you would treasure! You encouraged her as she learned and showed pride in her work. It deserved to be on the front of the fridge, right? I still keep those pictures, don't you?

Keep this metaphor in mind as you think through your team's attempts at taking on new and broader work than before. This empowerment thing isn't a linear progression either. It will take time, patience, persuasion and encouragement from you. They won't be perfect. But, with proper leadership, they will grow into it. Same for you, by the way.

But here's the rub. Kids (especially teenagers) and some employees for that matter, don't necessarily *want* to become fully functional adults. They have gotten used to passing their problems along to you to be solved. They are often quite satisfied if you keep doing so. In fact, they may prefer it this way; it gives them a built-in excuse for failure. After all, they just did what you told them to do, right? Have you ever heard them say, "I did exactly what you told me to do!" (Even if they knew at the time it was stupid.) Now what?

On the Other Side of the Coin ...

I had a boss named Ruby early in my career right out of grad school. I was just learning the ropes in the real world. She commissioned me to work on my first project and insisted that it be presented to her in a large, sealed envelope. Weird, I know.

When I brought it to her, she asked, *"Is this an example of your best work?" If so, I will open it now. If not, please take it back until you are confident that it is the best you can do. No harm, no foul".* OMG!

I was intimidated and vaguely fearful by her question. "What if she hates it", I wondered silently, Can I do better? Maybe. I'll look at it again. Somewhat sheepishly, I pulled it back across the table with one finger. "I guess I would like to review it one more time, Ruby", I said. Sure enough, her question prompted me to dig deeper than I normally would to find ways to improve my work.

Eventually, I had to present my work as the best I could do. I was so nervous that I couldn't sit still as she read through my work making pencil notes in the margin that I couldn't read. My mind was racing. "I knew it. She hates it", I thought.

Eventually she looked up over the reading glasses perched on the end of her nose and said, "Ken, this is truly outstanding work! I'm so proud to have you on my team! If you are open to it, I do have few minor suggestions which may be helpful from my vantage point. Would you be interested in reviewing them?"

Relieved, I replied, "Of course, I would; I'm here to learn". This was the beginning of a long and richly rewarding relationship I had with Ruby. She taught me so many, many things about work and about life while always treating me with dignity and respect, as an equal. Mostly I learned that I was capable of more than I knew. The whole team felt that way about her. That was her legacy.

Random Thought: Why Do People Get Shorter and Shorter by the Day?

Here's a weird phenomenon I have observed over and over again in almost every traditional organization. If you watch closely as folks come into work in the morning, they seem to get physically shorter right before our eyes! It's like the minute they walk slowly through the door, they shrink. Their shoulders droop and their heads slump. Oddly enough, when they leave for the day, they walk faster, stand taller and have more energy after a full day than when they started. What's going on here?

Here's my take on it. Out 'there' in the real world before and after work, they must be fully functioning adults. They have no choice. They raise kids; they manage money; they problem solve; they care for the elderly; they make investment decisions; they contribute to society; they coach soccer teams; they vote; and they do all manner of grown-up things. They have to. If they don't do this stuff, who will?

But, at work, those same skills, abilities and experience are not expected, required or even welcomed. They can become childlike in the following ways: they frequently ask for permission; they delegate problem-solving upward in the organization; they relinquish financial responsibility; they wait for the boss to decide things and submit readily to being 'managed'.

Sometimes you'll hear, "Somebody needs to do something about this!" That 'somebody' is usually you.

They have conformed to our perception of them that they need parents at work to tell them what to do, when to do it and how to do it. Their discretionary effort falls to zero while they shrug their shoulders and wait for you to decide what to do. They wait until you provide them with answers, with decisions and with solutions. In short, they become like kids again at work. This becomes a self-fulfilling cycle after a while. You get the picture.

How did this happen? In the United States at least, if not Western countries in general, we have followed the 'command-and-control' dogma that we were raised under. We were taught the rightness of it. We were measured against it. We were rewarded for it, as I said earlier. Here's the kicker: We are now leaders BECAUSE we followed it. We bought into it. We make lots of money and enjoy all the perks and power associated with it. That's just our paradigm.

I readily submit that, even though we have built the most successful economy in human history, the command-and-control system that we have been practicing has also produced the undesirable side effect of employees who check their brains, passion, creativity, experience and talents at the door.

I know this is a hard pill to swallow. Just like parents, we want the best for our kids. We want them to be successful. We want to remove stress and the risk of failure for them. Our motives are pure. Nevertheless, we have unintentionally stunted their growth. They are functioning at a fraction of their capability.

Story Time: *Why Do You Hate That Guy?*

I had a potential lean transformation client, who was considering me as his primary consultant. He took me on a tour of his large manufacturing facility. They produced automotive lubricants and other liquid chemicals. With great pride, the plant manager, Frank, showed me all the wonderful machines and people at work. He even bragged about being the best in the industry. I was impressed. Indeed, all the pieces seemed to be in place for them to be truly world class. But something was wrong, and he knew it. We both did. He could feel it, but he couldn't quite put his finger on it.

Near the end of the tour, we came upon a worker, Dan, who told me he had worked there for over 30 years. His job, he explained, was to pull out the occasional and random empty plastic containers that somehow made it through the production line without being properly filled. He would then strip the outer labels off from them and toss them into a big bin to be recycled. Then he would wait until another one came along. He did this perfectly and effortlessly. He was obviously proud of his company and his role in it.

As we went on with the tour and out of earshot from Dan, I asked Frank, "Why do you hate that guy so much?" He looked at me as if to say, 'HUH?' "Why is he being punished?" I pressed. He then said, "Punished? No way! He's one of our best, most senior guys! And that is one of the most desirable jobs in the whole place. He is at the top of the wage scale, too!" Visibly annoyed, he then asked me, "Why would you even think that?"

I then asked him, "I'm just wondering what a good day would look like for Dan? When he went home, what would he have to say about how his day went over the dinner table? Would it be something like, "hey Honey, I set a new record. I recycled 1,233 empty bottles today! Maybe I'll get a bonus!'"

I could see the look on Frank's face as the blood drained from it. Suddenly he realized what I was saying. He immediately grasped that, not only was he 'rewarding' his best worker with meaningless work, but he had also institutionalized waste into his production line to boot. He was systematically robbing one of his best workers of the chance to learn, to grow, to take risks, to problem solve … to be a grown up.

He realized that there were probably a LOT more Dans there who were utterly disengaged from their work and wholly disconnected from the mission of the company. He was rewarding people by giving them work that was mind numbing and repetitive with no challenge or opportunity to grow.

Not much was said as we walked back to his office. It was an awkward silence, but I could almost hear his mind working, spinning in overdrive as he tried to process this new epiphany. He was doing some deep soul searching (or as we say in lean speak, Hansei). "How did I not see this?" he later shared.

At least now he had begun to grasp why his plant, although 'best-in-class', had plateaued. They had become, *the cream of the crap* and he knew it. He wondered how much more he might accomplish with actively engaged, problem-solving adults who could contribute like true partners in the enterprise.

I got the contract.

The good news is that we know how to remedy this. We teach kids to ride bikes, don't we? We start with the training wheels firmly planted on the ground. We then gradually raise them, adding a degree of risk in the process, until we ultimately remove them altogether. Yes, we accept that they may well crash into a parked car, but we are there for them when they do. We know that failure is a part of learning. We help them figure out what went wrong and encourage them to try again, right? Why wouldn't this work in your organization? Your Lean coach will be an enormous help here.

Reflection Questions

- Are you so busy protecting your employees and staff that you have systematically removed the opportunity for them to fail, learn and grow?
- What *really* happens in your organization when the team tries and fails at new things?
- Is it safe there to say, "I don't know how to do ABC?"
- Do you have adult expectations of your employees?
- Are they becoming interdependent, fully functioning, self-confident, problem-solving adults at work as they must be at home?
- Do you willingly accept problems that are delegated upward to you?

Chapter 9

Key Lean Leader Behaviors

As stated earlier, there are a few key differences between what traditional managers do vs. lean leaders. Here are of few of the most significant differences (Figure 9.1).

So ...

1. Get out of your office!
2. Go to where the work is being done (gemba) and observe what is actually happening firsthand.
3. Ask front line workers what inhibits their ability to perform their work easily and smoothly. What obstacles do they experience that are beyond their control?
4. Listen and learn. Ask questions from a perspective of curiosity vs. judgment.
5. Resist the temptation to solve problems but encourage those closest to problems to try out their own ideas.
6. Remove barriers. Help clarify which problems MUST be solved, those blocking progress toward strategic objectives. Focus on RELEVANT problems and redirect energy from meaningless problem-solving exercises.
7. Focus everyone, everywhere on the customer; confirm that they can articulate who their customers are, internal and/or external.
8. Relentlessly attack waste and mind-numbing repetition.

Traditional Managers	Lean Leaders
Conduct work in offices, on phones and in conference rooms	Go to gemba to see and learn firsthand what is actually happening
Use authority to govern and force adherence to policy	Use data and experience to coach for improvement, growth and learning
Fear failure	Embrace failure as a means to learn and grow
Make decisions	Encourage thinking and risk assessment
Solve problems	Role model problem solving methodology
Answer questions	Ask Socratic, thought provoking questions
Rely on experience and hunch	Rely on facts and data
Fight fires	Prevent fires
Treat symptoms	Eliminate root causes

Figure 9.1

In Figure 9.2a, the team member is surrounded by rocks and boulders representing problems to be solved. She is asking which problems she should attack first. Should she start with smaller ones to get some quick wins? Or should she dive into big ones to get something significant accomplished? Does she need a shovel or a backhoe? There are problems everywhere she looks!

"Just start digging! Don't bring me problems; bring me solutions!" we say. From this perspective, without any other input or direction, this approach seems to work equally well either way.

OK, now let's add a goalpost (Figure 9.2b). See also "Hoshin Kanri". This changes everything! Suddenly, it becomes obvious where to start. Solve the

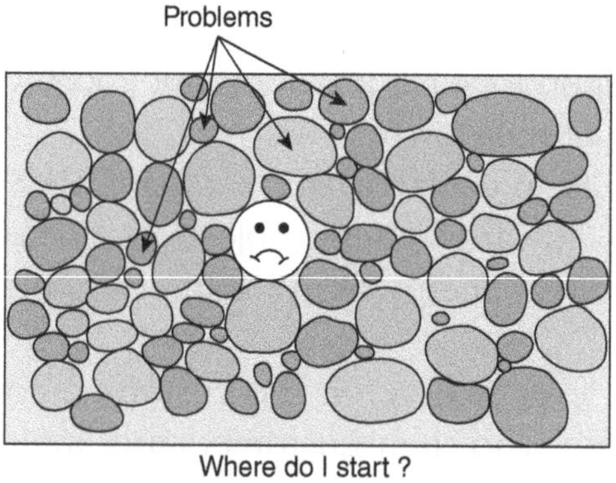

Figure 9.2a

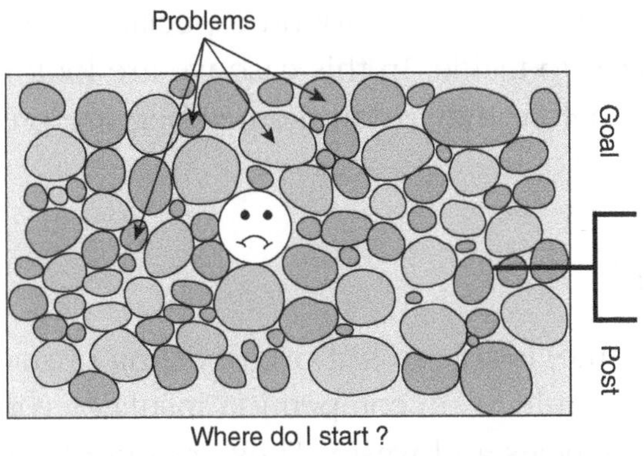

Figure 9.2b

problems that *must* be solved and remove any obstacles between you and your goal! Focus! Stop solving problems that are irrelevant.

Identify which problems can be solved at each of the various levels in the organization. The team usually can solve the smaller ones within their normal domain and call on you and others to remove the bigger or more cross-organizational ones.

In Figure 9.2c, the direction set now illuminates the pathway and renders all other problems secondary or completely irrelevant. Highlight the problems and barriers *between your current state and your future state.*

Help illuminate the goal and empower your teams to figure out how to get there! Most importantly, stop work that doesn't get you to your goal! Free up those resources to focus on the right work. This is a major role of the lean leader!

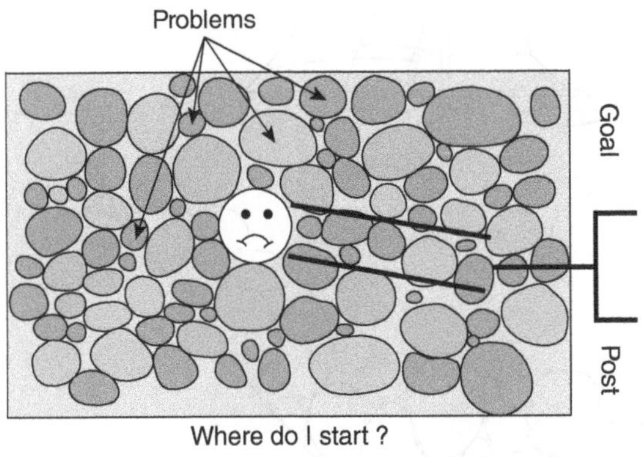

Figure 9.2c

Here's another image that I have found especially useful to help decide what problems I need to tackle. In this case we are looking ahead to anticipate problems before they occur. Remember, fire prevention is better than firefighting!

Will We Make It?

Your boat, the SS Acme, is able to sail over existing obstacles (Figure 9.3). Maybe high prices or little to no competition insulates you from unseen obstacles like inefficiencies and waste. They are out of sight below the waterline. But will you be able to clear the rocks ahead as you sail into shallower water? Maybe the economy has caused you to lower your prices? Maybe there's new competition coming? What other threats may cause you to run aground if you don't take decisive action?

Two Strategies

1. Lighten your load to raise the boat (eliminate waste) by dumping ballast-like projects that aren't really relevant anymore.
2. Elevate your perspective and look ahead to mitigate obstacles that may cause you to run aground. Do your research.
   a. What's the competition doing?
   b. What new or changing technology might have an impact on you?

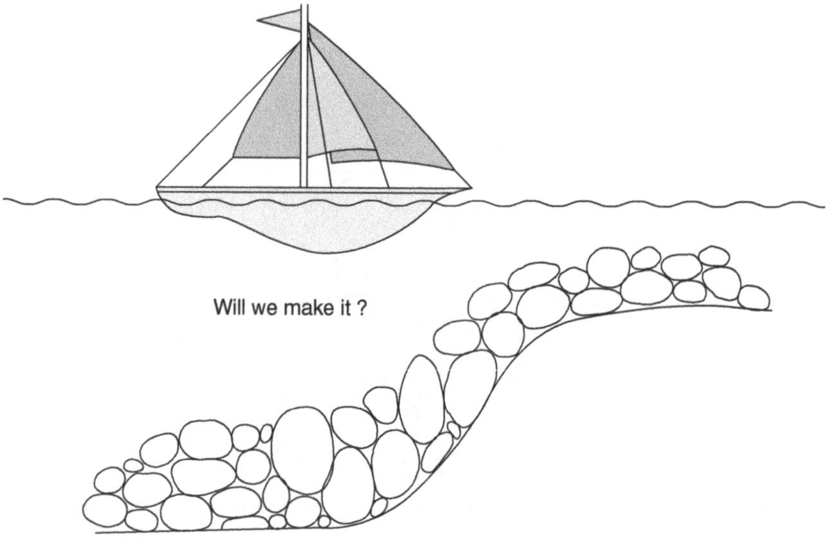

Figure 9.3

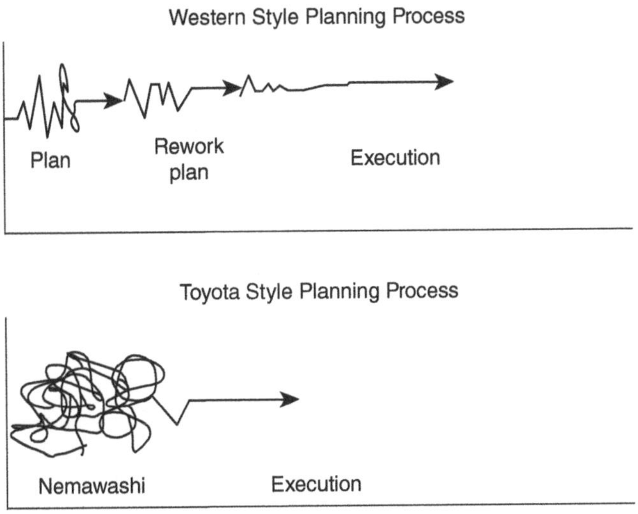

Figure 9.4

c. What other market forces, i.e., the economy, might be a risk to you?
d. What might be coming down the pike (i.e., changing the legal landscape)?
e. Do either politics or elections have any bearing on us?
f. Is it time to conduct a deep SWAT analysis?

Two Different Ways to Plan

This is a depiction I often use to compare and contrast lean, Toyota-style planning and execution cycles to traditional, Western styles.

The top drawing (Figure 9.4) represents several iterations from planning to execution over time. The amplitude of the planning phases is reduced over time after experience informs us of what is working and what isn't. Think warranty work here.

The bottom drawing depicts the more extensive lean-based planning and testing that Toyota does BEFORE anything gets executed. This prevents rework while also maximizing buy-in and confidence in the product or service before releasing it to the customer. Again, think nemawashi.

Chapter 10

What's the One Thing?

Random Thought

Do you take multi-vitamins? Why? Traditionally, people will say, "Because I need them." OK, but which exact vitamin do *YOU* need?" Is it C? D3? Iron? Zinc? Magnesium? My doctor asked me if I was taking multi-vitamins. I said "Yes, daily gummies". He said, "Stop". He went on to say, "From looking at your blood test results, all you really need is 1,000 mg of zinc daily". Hmmm...

Our custom is often to solve problems with what we in the United States call, the *shotgun approach.* We even have expressions in our language that tip us off to this habit like *Fire for effect; Ready, fire, aim*; *Throw everything including the kitchen sink at it;* or *I don't care how you get it done, just get it done!* Often we deploy additional and perhaps unnecessary people resources at problems than what we actually need.

Consider this: Why is a real double barrel shotgun useful? Simply put, the shotgun shell contains many individual 'shots' or pellets that spray out in a predetermined pattern. So, all we have to do to get our duck is to point in the general direction of the target, fire away and pray that one of the 100 pellets hits something. But which one? Where did the other 99 pellets go?

The biggest problem with the shotgun, or the shotgun approach for that matter, is that it works. Yes, the fact that it WORKS is the problem! Even though it is inherently wasteful, we default to it. Why? We have grooved a certain way of doing things that produces results often without question.

Could it be that we just aren't very good at aiming? This is a cornerstone of lean. Aiming. If we learn to aim well, we can squeeze off one single rifle shot to get our duck.

But, how did we find ourselves here? We are a nation of limitless abundance. Think about it; when was the last time we ran out of anything? Because we are a nation of bounty, we have developed some assumptions and habits that may be getting in our way. We assume that there will always be more resources when we need them. Think Costco.

We have unconsciously fallen into the trap of *more is better*. But is it? If COVID has taught us anything, it is that we may yet have to adapt to shortages. We saw hoarding of basic supplies because for the first time, we wondered if the supplies we needed would actually be there when we needed them. This is a new phenomenon for many of us! This is the norm in Venezuela, not here!

Other parts of the world do not have the luxury of abundance or limitless natural resources. So, by extension, they have had to learn to aim better; to use what they have available. Since they don't have bountiful resources in the first place, squandering them is not an option. You could say that they are purposely stingy when using resources. Measure twice; cut once.

Enter Toyota. Emerging from just such an environment of resource scarcity, they arose. Toyota, existing as it does in the Japanese natural resource-limited environment, quite naturally deployed their resources only after considerable thought and a thorough analysis of the various options available. Once a course of action was taken, the results of that action were quickly assessed for its impact. Put another way, if they missed the first time, they would take another shot, a single shot, then adjust accordingly prior to taking the next shot, and so on.

Here's the point. Toyota has extended its practice of using resources judiciously to include the use of its people and time resources as well. They analyze any action deeply before taking it. They study various options before picking one. In short, they aim very well.

Story Time: *What Can Curly Teach Us?*

So, what about us? What are we to do? We can take a lesson from Curly. If you have seen the movie "City Slickers", you will know the main character is a rough cowboy who owns a dude ranch. Curly, played magnificently by Jack Palance, shares wisdom with his novice dudes. If you haven't seen it, do so.

There is a scene in the movie where Curly is trying to help Billy Crystal, a city slicker, discover himself and to help him find meaning in his life.

Curly holds up his index finger in his black gloved hand from atop his horse, cigarette dangling from his mouth and says, "You need to figure out the one thing". Whereupon Billy asks Curly, "But what is the one thing?" To which Curly responds, "That's what you've got to figure out!" and rides off into the sunset. Brilliant.

In my office hangs a picture of this exact scene, with Curly holding up his index finger in his gloved hand. It's there to remind me constantly to search for the *one* right thing to do. Over time, I have learned to ask my clients, "What is the *next* one thing you need to do?" This can be a startling question. We have so internalized the notion of 'more is better' that we rarely dig any deeper than trying to fix nearly every problem using the tried-and-true shotgun approach.

Where's the Key Log?

In the early days of the logging industry, trees were cut down and dumped into the river (Figure 10.1). They were floated downstream to where they would be gathered up and brought to a waiting paper mill.

Inevitably, a logjam would occur along the way, thus stopping the flow of logs. Sometimes these logjams would be huge, many acres or more. The technology of the day was to set dynamite and blow up the jam until it was released, and the current would move the logs along to the next jam, where the process would be repeated. Along the way, a lot of valuable lumber was reduced to toothpicks, to say nothing about the effect on the poor fish below.

Eventually, a new technology emerged, in this case a helicopter with a hook dangling underneath. From that higher vantage point, 'key logs' could be more easily spotted. These are the logs that got stuck somehow along the way, causing the backup. Once they found the key log(s), they could then lift it up and out and deposit it downstream. In so doing, they saved a lot of lumber *and* preserved the environment!

The lesson here is inescapable. We need to shift our focus, our vantage point, to a higher level. We need to begin to challenge our habits and spend more time analyzing the actions we propose before taking them. Starting with the key questions: "Who is our customer?" and "What do they want?"

I don't cover it in depth here, but there is a parallel in the 2P/3P tool set called, the "7 Ways." It forces those reconsidering how to improve value streams in brown or green field environments to consider at least seven alternatives before zeroing in on one to try out.

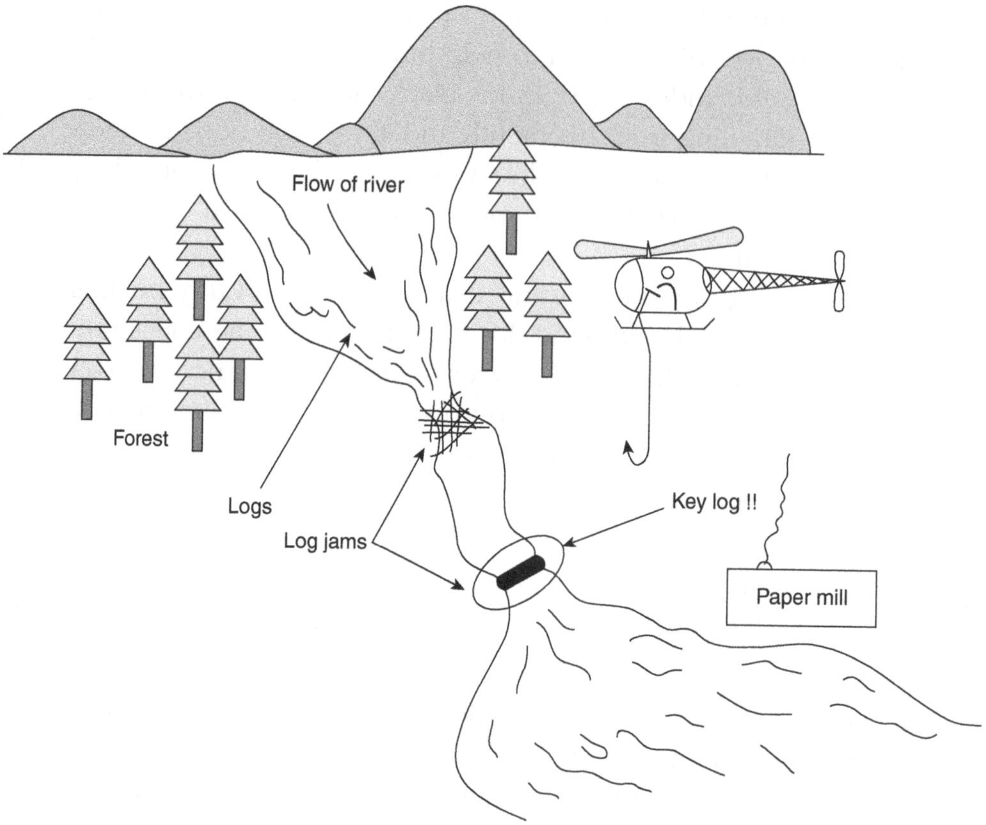

Figure 10.1

By the way, there is no magic in the number 7. Maybe five will do. The idea is to stretch your thinking to consider multiple actions before selecting the "next 1 thing" to do. Beware of the tendency to LOLO (lock on; lock out)! She is an evil mistress! This is a very common mistake. We pick somebody's favorite idea or pet project to implement, without serious consideration of other alternatives first.

It is hard for people to let go and keep considering other options once they have 'locked on' to the one they are convinced is 'the' answer. The seven ways is a discipline that can help break that habit.

Building an Operating System

One of the most important elements in your new lean enterprise will be the creation and management of your own operating system. Your coach will help immensely here to design and construct it, but the basics bones of the system are things like

- Establishment of overarching 'True North' Hoshins (high level ambitions; e.g., modernization)
- Alignment of goals and objectives at the value stream level
- Alignment of daily work via performance boards and daily tiered huddles
- Creation of visual management systems
- Development of an escalation process
- A kata-based development system
- A deliberate process of sunsetting 'wrong' work
- Building of a tiered reporting structure
- A kaizen methodology
- Designing a 5S strategy
- Possibly a physical restructuring of various workspaces
- Alignment of HR-related functions (e.g., recruiting, reward and promotion systems)
- Deliberate and thorough training of all hands, especially middle management, and supervision

Daily Management

There will need to be a robust daily management system built. This is quite literally where the rubber meets the road. I can assess the maturity of a 'lean organization' in one stop at the daily performance huddles and performance displays. In that one place, I can determine how healthy the operating system for that value stream is immediately. It will show me most, if not all, of the elements bulleted above. As a leader, you will be able to determine what each team needs from you, if anything, right there.

Chapter 11

What's Next?

Let's go back to the beginning and dive deeper into the first phase of the lean transformation, *Introduction*. This is where all the heavy lifting occurs as the gravitational pull from prior 'flavor-of-the-month' cynicism kicks in. It will require uncommon persistence to overcome it, but it can be done.

Just remember that your folks are skeptical for a reason! They have learned that they can usually ride out the latest management fad. Most will give you lip service that they're on board but, trust me on this, beneath the surface, resistance is alive and well. Once they begin to see that this is all about common sense, they will begin to come out of hiding and play along. Don't be surprised when you hear, "It's about time!" or, "I've been telling you this for years!" from many.

Keeping It Real

TIP: Be realistic both with yourself and with your team. This *will* require extra work early in the journey. Be honest about it! It will be additive to the work you and your organization are already doing, too. Think of home remodeling. Why would anybody in their right mind undertake such a thing? It's messy, expensive and hugely disruptive. This drawing may help you illustrate the point to your teams to set realistic but hopeful expectations.

From this image, Figure 11.1, you can see that you are currently working say, eight to ten hours per day (Column 1). When you begin your lean journey in the *Introduction* phase, you will have to accept that the new work will be added on top of the old work (Column 2). But, as time goes by,

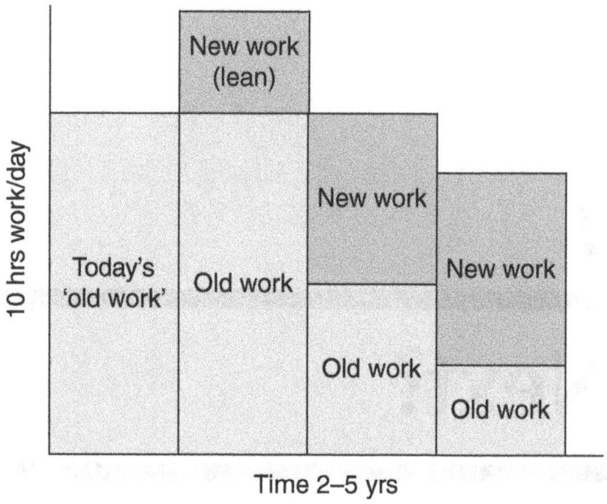

Figure 11.1

the new work will begin to replace old work, as newly empowered people and teams begin to solve problems, etc., below you (Column 3); this is the work that YOU used to do.

Eventually, you will finally have the time to do that thing at work that you have always wanted to do but never had time for (Column 4). You will experience something quite unfamiliar: Extra time. Imagine that!

By the way, do you know what they call work that has no deadline? A hobby. That important work that you have never been able to complete sits idly in your inbox. Why? No deadline. Sure, it's important but you never quite have enough time to do it. This is your hobby work.

Meanwhile, less important but 'urgent' work devours all your time and attention! But, as the shift gradually occurs, you will begin to find that not only are you doing more of the important work you always intended to do but you will be happier than ever doing it. You will finally be working, as they say in healthcare, at the top of your license!

Ultimately, you must keep reminding yourself and others how much better things will be when you're done. This is where you, the leader, come in. This is where you need to set a clear and compelling vision of what it will be like when you arrive 'there'. People need to 'see' the future and get excited about creating it. Paint the picture for them in vivid colors! Always begin with the end in mind!

Your passion, clarity, patience and persistence will be fully taxed. Nobody wants to follow a leader who doesn't know where she is going. This is Leadership 101! Create in your own mind how much better the place will be after you have truly transformed into a lean, agile and customer-focused company. Once you have 'seen' it yourself, you will be able to excite others about it, too.

Random Thought: I Can See Things That Don't Exist

Biologists and anthropologists tell us that, as far as we know, we are the only creatures who can create something that does not currently exist. We're not talking here about birds building nests or spiders spinning webs. Those are instinctive behaviors. What I am talking about here is the human ability to 'see' that which doesn't exist and then set about creating it.

Look around you now. Everything around you started as somebody's original idea. The computer I'm writing from didn't arise from the ground. We invented it. We saw it first in our minds, then we created it. We even say we can see something in our "mind's eye".

Can you imagine a pink, polka-dotted killer whale? Of course, you can. Even though it doesn't exist! This ability to visualize seems to be uniquely human. Why not use it? You can create what you can imagine. This is the origin of art, science, engineering, innovation, invention, mathematics, architecture, music and even this book! We can create by using only our 'vision', that which doesn't yet exist but one day WILL!

Find your early adopters and work with them. They are your 'sparkplugs'. Don't waste your time with the folks that will never be first to try anything. They are your anchors. They are slow to excite and habitually negative. Somewhere in your organization there are those folks just itching to try something new, find them. They're at the right side of your performance bell curve.

Pull them in and excite them with your vision. Eventually, the middle folks in the bell curve will come around once they see some progress. So, create a wake! After all, who wants to be part of an organization that never moves forward anyway? Of course, the faster you go, the bigger the wake of disruption you will cause. But what's the alternative? You could stay still, drop anchor and make no wake at all. Sound like fun? Not to me.

A Slow Ride to Nowhere

What if Disneyland created and spent millions of dollars on developing a new ride. It would be flat and travel in a straight line at 4 mph with nothing to see on either side but a blank wall. Maybe they could call it "Yawn". Sound fun? I don't think the line to ride it would be awfully long, at least. We want excitement, adventure, thrill, stimulation and even some degree of perceived risk, don't we? Your journey should be the same.

The anchors in your bell curve will come along eventually. They will make themselves known to you. You'll know them by things they say like, "Let me play devil's advocate" or "I have done this before, and it didn't work". Look back occasionally to see if they are starting to wake up. If they do, be quick to acknowledge them and be mildly empathetic with their learned skepticism. But don't, I repeat, DON'T reward them with too much attention. Save that for the sparkplug folks. Alas, the old bell curve is always present. Work with it.

Decision Time

Based on all of the above, it's time to decide. Is this a venture worth pursuing? **CAUTION**: If you decide to dive in, there's no real turning back without creating more problems than you started with. From my own experience, I would honestly say that, if you proceed with enthusiasm, passion and purpose, you will never regret it.

Get out there. Your primary consultant can give you a list of places to visit to see lean in action for yourself in other places. Take your hand-picked team of sparkplugs there with you. You will come home convinced and eager to put your shovel in the ground.

Yes, there will be challenges to be sure. You will fail, as I have. Everybody does. You will pick yourself up and start again. And yes, you *will* succeed. Be transparent with your team. Chances are that they will be just as determined as you are if they are included in the creation of this great journey together from the get-go.

An axiom that I remind myself of frequently, *People don't care how much you know until they know how much you care.* Lead with your passion; don't fear it. It will be contagious. This is the stuff of real leaders. Look at Elon Musk!

If you decide to take the next step, there are abundant resources to help get you there. A word of caution: do your due diligence before selecting a transformation consultant/partner. There are many good ones but some hacks are out there, too. Research them thoroughly and choose them thoughtfully. You are entrusting your company's culture and your own reputation to them. They won't come cheap. But remember that this is an investment in your future.

You don't really have to invest a lot on consulting costs over the long term. Good consultants with real experience can help you see how you will gain more in increased productivity (cost/unit), lower operating costs, higher morale, improved teamwork, enhanced flexibility and reduced turnover than you will ever spend!

The payback is real and nearly immediate. Get your HR and accounting teams involved early on as a reality check. I am always amazed at how much companies save vs. what they spend. But be careful NOT to sell lean to make more money, or especially, do NOT EVER introduce this as a cost-cutting measure! If you do, you will be done before you start.

Yes, you will reduce costs, but that is the inevitable outcome of this work, not the purpose of it. If you talk about lean to reduce cost or to lower overhead, guess what your people will hear? Layoffs! You must find the will and the support from HR, the board and all senior leaders to tell them UPFRONT that there will NOT be layoffs because of this work.

You must promise them that, in the event that positions are eliminated or combined, displaced people WILL be retained, perhaps in new and even better jobs that they help create! If you don't make this promise, do NOT start this process! Stop now. Your investment in this book will have been worth it if it prevents you from starting off on the wrong foot.

Keep this in mind throughout. Properly executed, lean is genuinely an investment in every sense of the word, and not an expense! You may very well see savings more than ten times what you invest! This is a very low estimate, too. Check it out for yourself. But I repeat, do NOT start out with a cost-savings goal. Savings will be the result of your work. It is not the point of it.

Importantly, if the word gets out that this is just the latest cost-cutting scheme, you will have a hard time overcoming that presumption. I recommend even distancing yourself from cost-reduction successes conspicuously at first.

Again, re-stress that this is NOT about cost savings or ROI. This is about creating a new value in a renewed customer-focused enterprise with on-fire people! Of course, as you expose and minimize waste, savings will surely follow. Say nothing more in this domain for now.

This is a big deal. Do yourself a favor and take the time to mull it over. Change is hard. Even good changes are traumatic but well worth the effort. Sometimes you have to go slow in the short run so you can go fast later.

Random Thought: Who Needs Brakes?

Do you know why they put brakes on cars? So that you can go fast! Think about it.

Chapter 12

A Sneak Preview into Part 2—Integration

Note: What follows is a glimpse into some of the topics we will discuss in my next book *Part 2—Integration.* The below will give you just a peek over the horizon on what comes next if you decide to take the lean transformation leap. This is just a sampling, but it will give you a sense of the next phase of your journey.

As we discussed in Phase 1, "Introduction", the heavy lifting occurs as you are trying to get this culture change started. Like a Saturn 5 rocket, most of the energy consumed is merely to get the thing off the ground and to overcome gravitational pull. Your gravitational pull will be from the fear of change, cynicism, habits, norms and a stubborn, inflexible corporate culture.

Most of your work, the maximum level of effort required, occurs in Phase 1. As we discussed in Part 1, recall the law of physics from high school: *Objects at rest tend to remain at rest; objects in motion tend to remain in motion.* But here, in Phase 2 "Integration" is where you will be at the greatest risk of failure because you are at the tipping point. If you relax too early, you will lose your momentum and fall back. Think of this as the Stage 2 rocket that can get you into orbit. Or in foot races, don't run TO the tape, run THROUGH it!

As Winston Churchill put it, "Success consists of going from failure to failure without losing enthusiasm". The tipping point may be reached, but there is no guarantee at all that it will tip in the right direction! Many a transformation has fallen backward over itself only to make it ten times harder to resurrect the next time you try.

So, "Integration", while requiring less raw energy, is fraught with hazards. This is where you will encounter resistance of a different kind. It's one thing to get your staff all jazzed up about the new culture in the abstract, but quite another when you start to tinker with the organization's fundamental fabric. A vision is, by nature, abstract. Now we are making real, tangible changes.

You will be making changes to policy, to job descriptions, to hiring practices, to leadership behaviors, to planning, to execution, to product development, to shareholder value, etc., etc., etc. This is where transforming your culture becomes real for people. Consider the axiom, *Change is great; you go first!*

This is not for the faint of heart. The good news is that, if you have created enough enthusiasm and sheer inertia, it will help propel you through the murky realm of integration. A good place to start is when you are introducing a new value stream or perhaps the areas of greatest need for reorganization efforts.

Remember: Hold fast to the vision. Constantly remind your team that you are going to the promised land! Always keep it in sharp focus. Just like home remodeling, having a picture on the refrigerator of the way it's going to look like can help through the worst times. *Hang in there* becomes a daily mantra. As hard as you try to anticipate every detail, you will learn that any time you do something new, it *WILL* be ugly!

At some point you will have half the company doing business in the old way while the other half is trying to do it the new way, not easy. You are neither a caterpillar nor a butterfly now. You will be in a very precarious, vulnerable and otherwise uncomfortable place. Find joy in the journey and trust the process, yourself and your consultant. You will emerge with wings spread. Reminding the team relentlessly about the future state will help soothe them somewhat.

Random Thought: What's Happening to Me?

I like to compare this process to cosmetic plastic surgery. In the lobby of plastic surgeons' offices, it is typical to see before and after photo binders of prior patients. But in one office, as a consultant, not as a patient, I saw a set of pictures showing pictures taken in the *during* phase, not pretty, why?

If you saw only the before and after pictures, you might freak out about the swelling, bruising and pain that occurs inevitably between those two points of reference. By sharing the pictures in mid-process, the patient may still be very anxious but at least she can say, "Well, at least the surgeon told me that I should expect this; 'it's normal', he said".

The same goes here. If you paint too rosy a picture of the end state and gloss over the disruption and inevitable ugliness, your teams will freak out when it happens. Be honest, candid and transparent.

At least when it happens, you can reassure them that it is a normal part of the 'remodeling process'. A good, seasoned consultant will earn his/her fees here! To you, I offer this quote, "Calm seas never made an expert sailor".

Help them focus when there is more than one issue at hand to be resolved. You'll hear exaggerated statements like, "This place is a mess" or "Nobody knows what to do next" or "I liked it better the old way". This is clear evidence that you need to help them isolate ONE issue at a time. Fix that issue and then move on to the others.

Would you agree that improvement = change? If so, then continuous improvement must = continuous change. And, therefore, continuous change equates to continuous resistance. Or, to put it more simply, continuous improvement will naturally be met with continuous resistance! But, if you're not changing things, you are a caretaker, not a leader.

Your Role in Leading Change

Let's review in Figure 12.1 an example of how change is typically 'processed' by individuals as well as groups.

Box 1: You and/or your company are static. This is the status quo. You are typically neither really happy nor really sad. Just content with the way things are. *Your job here*: Force change; disrupt complacency; start a fire on the platform.

Box 2: The organization and the people in it will likely push back. Even though they didn't love things before, they were familiar. *Your job here*: Empathize and press forward.

Box 3: Once they realize the change is inevitable, they will fall into apparent dysfunction. *Your job here*: Help them clarify what isn't working in *detail* and fix one problem at a time.

Box 4: They're starting to understand it. They see the new world taking shape, the light at the end of the tunnel. *Your job here*: Celebrate with them. Enjoy the moment and then start another fire.

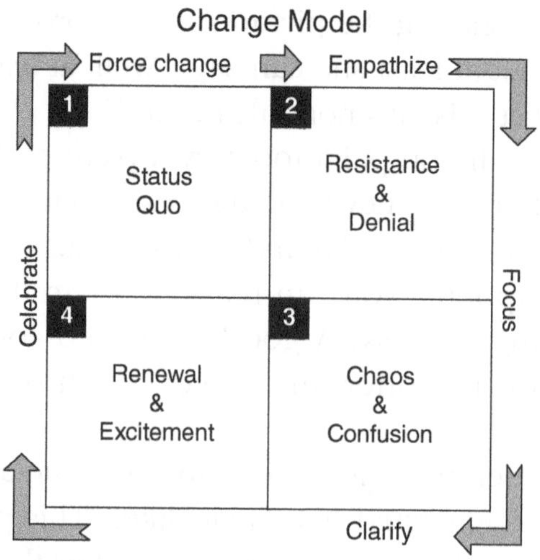

Figure 12.1

Random Thought: Cement Mixers

Did you ever notice that the big drum on a cement truck is always rotating, albeit slowly, even when driving down the road? Why is that? What if it stopped? Then what? This is an apt metaphor for continuous improvement. If you stop, your organization will begin to 'set up' like concrete.

Key Functions and Relationships to Develop

Note: These are only a few of the more obvious common company departments to consider. Your consultant partner will work with you to identify others that are relevant to your circumstances.

HR

As the leader of your organization, you will be in the driver's seat throughout the transformation process. You are the pilot. But, as critical as that is, you will still need the counsel of some key players in your corner. You need a navigator. None is more important to your success than HR. They will be your eyes and ears. It is vital that you have confidence in their abilities beyond their traditional roles and responsibilities. Ideally, they will already have Organization Development (OD) resources in their department.

If not, ask them what capabilities they will need to ensure you have strong INTERNAL OD (Change Management) support.

You don't want to have a lean consultant around forever, no matter how good they may be. I had a client refer to his prior consulting company as "The barnacles". Every time he tried to end the relationship with them, they quickly 'discovered' something new for him to do or a new tool that they wanted to introduce.

The antidote to this is to build internal capability in the "Integration" phase. Consider having a clause in your lean consulting contract that specifies a key deliverable to build a Lean Promotion Office (LPO), aka Kaizen Dept., etc., to help you staff it and to train the people in it. As you learn more and more, you should be able to wean yourself gradually from external sources. Think relay race. Your contract should have an expiration date with an option to renew.

In my contracts, I specify that around mid-term in my work, we will consciously begin to build internal capacity and capability. We built the plane; they will fly it. While I strongly recommend that the LPO Director report directly to the CEO/President, it will still require HR support and planning to make it happen.

10 Specific Questions You'll Need to Address with HR

1. What is the potential impact on the workforce?
2. How do I gain support from the union?
3. How are the reward systems aligned (or not) around this model?
4. Do we recognize heroics around here? Firefighting vs. fire prevention?
5. Do we care as much about how work is done as we do about the end results?
6. What is the current readiness of our existing leaders?
7. Who are likely to be the early adopters?
8. How should we change our recruiting practices to attract the 'right' people?
9. How should we deal with the employees and managers who won't or can't change?
10. What kind of training, development and OD capability do we have?

Remember: HR is a *KEY* stakeholder in this process. With their enthusiastic support, you can make steady progress. Without it, tough sledding is ahead.

Manufacturing and Other Front-Line Employees

They will experience the biggest and most conspicuous changes. They will be EXPECTED to stop the line when a defect occurs. They will fail and freak out. This is a big culture shift. Be sure to reward those who DO stop the line quickly! There will be a lot of apprehension about this at first. As we discussed earlier, be extra careful about the readiness and enthusiasm from your middle management teams. One weak link in the management chain from lead person to VP can doom the transformation. Use your lean consultant to test the strength of that management team.

Engineering and Design

Like sales and marketing, they will have to learn to become more customer-centric vs. competition-centric. They will also have to learn to accept input from manufacturing, sales and marketing, quality and front-line workers AND customers. They will need to be included in work teams with unfamiliar people and processes. Focus groups will take on a new importance. They may need to be reinvented to solicit design and engineering input that you haven't even considered.

Story Time: *After the Echo*

The Echo was a product originally intended to compete with the Honda Civic, which was a favorite among young male 'tuners' because it was easy and cheap to customize. Ultimately, however, the Echo ended up appealing to the opposite demographic, mature women, instead. You couldn't have missed the mark more if you tried!

After the Echo debacle, Toyota reflected deeply on its market failure. They discovered that the root cause of the problem was that they had used their own team of very senior marketing executives to design a product intended for young tuners on skimpy budgets. They decided that their next stab at it would include the target buyers every step of the way from concept to design, to manufacturing, to sales, and even to service. They would have their own dealer network. It would have its own brand and even its own unique logo.

The results were legendary. From the ashes of Echo came Scion. It was an incredible market hit in every respect. For example, Scion had the first ever dedicated car club, the fastest growing club in history, before the cars were even introduced. There were rallies and special events BEFORE the car was even on sale. When they started selling, there were dedicated, "Scion Owners Only" pavilions! They even had unique vehicle design elements that were driven by the young first-time car customers who were the target buyers.

Can you imagine them saying to the engineers, "We want colored lights that shine down on our feet while we drive and a huge subwoofer in the trunk". Wait, what? But, true to their commitment, the company acquiesced to their requests and produced the car that THEY wanted!

Point made.

Quality

Be careful here. Quality typically is 'added in' at the final step. Lean is all about built-in quality and checking work before it leaves Station 1 on its way to Station 2, etc. Often, quality departments push back on lean as they THINK it jeopardizes the importance of their jobs. This is a false assumption. Their role will shift, however, to become more of a 'process' inspector vs. a 'product' inspector. They will also become primary coaches.

Much of their work currently involves a large inventory of things to be fixed! This will disappear over time and the department resources will, and should, be devoted to ensuring that defects stop at the point of cause (POC). Nowadays, I suspect most of your quality folks will have a good grasp of lean already.

Supply Chain

Moving from batch production to a seamless 'one-piece' flow will change the way you order materials and supplies. Some of your traditional suppliers will balk at this. Using your buying power leverage may help them to 'experiment' alongside you. You'll both learn a lot. Ultimately, you will see raw materials, parts, etc., arriving at your docks in smaller, 'line side' lots on a more frequent 'milk run' basis. Instead of large, wasteful warehouses, you will see suppliers filling min-max *kanbans*. Some suppliers like Grainger, for instance, already are geared up to meet the needs of their lean clients differently from their traditional clients.

Story Time: *Toyota and the Canadian Pacific Railway (CPR)*

I was asked to visit CPR to consult with them on how to reduce in-transit vehicle damage. We wanted our vehicles tied down inside rail cars differently from the way they tied down our competitors' products. They balked at having to have two different methods. "Why do you guys always have to be different?" They asked defiantly.

I told them that our preferred method will result in fewer carrier-damage-related insurance claims against them, a big reduction in paperwork and fewer process checks to ensure that our vehicles were handled correctly. I then said the magic words, "Hey, why don't we *experiment* with this new method *together* for a few months. If it works, you can then suggest that all your other customers would benefit from it equally and you would once again have the single system you want? If it doesn't, we will just return to the old way. Deal?"

Reluctantly, they agreed. After all, we had substantial buying power and they knew it. More importantly, we *never reminded them about it.* We never leveraged our dominant position to get what we wanted. We merely tried to find common ground and demonstrated our sincere desire to work closely with them to arrive at a win–win solution.

It worked. We established teams from both companies working together, side by side to accomplish an innovative tie-down process and tools that virtually eliminated in-transit damage, which CPR then spread to all its other customers. They achieved drastic cost improvements by reducing their damage claims, repair payouts and delayed sales by over 75%!

I'll never forget the comment made at the conclusion of our project in the *Hansei* (lessons learned) reflections as captured on our A3. One of the CPR team members said, "We have this love/hate thing going on with Toyota. We love that you always challenge us to improve but we hate that it's never good enough!" We all nodded in agreement. We agreed that we needed to stop saying, in effect, "Your end of the canoe is sinking". We came to appreciate that we're in this together with each other.

Random Thought: Howdy Pardner!

Did you know that the word "partner" is actually a contraction of the words "Part" and "Owner"? Over the years, those words became the slang "pardner" in the colonies. Violating the King's English in such an egregious fashion forced the creation of the new word "partner". Worth rediscovering the original concept when we think about work partners today.

Finance and Accounting

Careful here: thin ice ahead! Accountants and related finance professionals tend to get squirmy when you start talking about 'changing the culture'. Likewise, they are trained to sniff out BS cost savings. Nevertheless, they are a key part of your transformation and their commitment is crucial. It is important to stress that while your work *will* produce savings, that will be as a byproduct of improving processes and removing waste.

Also, and this is fundamental, let your accounting executives express their legitimate concerns. I have learned not to try to 'sell' the culture change but rather to ask them what they think the benefits, both financial and otherwise, might be to the organization. Once they grapple with it, you will most likely earn their support. Just don't shove it down their throats. This will backfire for sure!

A strong recommendation here: Include reps from Finance and Accounting in as many improvement projects as possible, even those from other unrelated projects.

Note: These are roles we refer to as 'outside eyes' and should be present at all kaizen events. They will become champions of lean in the process and bring priceless credibility to the team's work.

It IS important to categorize the benefits into hard and soft savings but not by you. Leave that claim to the teams themselves. Hard savings will come directly from reductions in inventory, space, material use, manpower redeployments, increased sales, etc. Soft savings will come about from reduced turnover, higher per person productivity, reduced absenteeism, etc. This is the time to remind them that you will NOT be stressing cost savings or staff reductions as the purpose of the transformation!

No matter what you do, some people will see it as cost cutting anyway but don't feed that notion. Dig deep and be bold enough to declare openly and publicly that there will NOT be any layoffs or RIFs as a direct result of this work. Print it, sign it and put it on a poster in the break room for all to see! Even with that conspicuous and public commitment, there will still be skepticism, but that will allow you to reinforce your promises and continuously remind them of it.

CAUTION: Do NOT, I repeat, do NOT use this transformation as an excuse to rid yourself of low performers, as tempting as that may be! Your commitment must be to everyone. Once again, this is where your HR partners can help.

Now let me speak out of the other side of my mouth for a moment. Some of your bottom performing employees may see this as a free pass to slack off. They may try to test your commitment not to lay anybody off as a result of your lean transformation work.

Remember that performance is *not negotiable* either with or without this change. While this may seem like you are backpedaling on your commitment, you aren't! If you have employees that are already marginal and maybe even on improvement plans, stick with those improvement plans. They may try to leverage your lean transformation to get off the hook, so to speak.

This is the right you retain to manage your workforce, union or union-free, and nothing about this process will take that away. But you MUST separate individual performance issues from redeployments stemming from streamlining processes. Your consultant will help and work with HR and legal counsel in this domain. Do not make a move without them!

Bottom line here is that you MUST gain the commitment of your Accounting and Finance department execs and staff. Without their skin in the game, you will risk losing credibility and momentum very quickly.

Sales and Marketing

Recall that earlier we spoke of being customer-centric. Typically, we sell 'to' customers rather than serving them on a deeper relationship level. There are often sales and marketing habits that must be changed or at least re-examined. It is common for the sales and marketing teams to focus on the competition rather than on the customer. While it may seem like we're splitting hairs here, there is a real difference.

Have your salespeople get out and actually SEE how the product and services you sell are being used by the consumer. Your competition might be trying to create a product 'enhancement' to have something to entice customers. Remember that just because you can do something, doesn't mean you should! Watch closely and observe how your customer uses your product and how aftermarket sales might inform you of their needs.

Story Time: *Watch Your Customers!*

Back in the day, before there were cup holders in cars, Toyota saw a trend toward aftermarket sales of cup hangers that you could hang from your car's windowsills. They saw that, even though customers weren't necessarily *asking* for cup holders directly, they were communicating by way of products needed to adapt their car to their unmet and unarticulated needs!

Another example was the creation of automatically opening sliding doors on vans. This came about from Toyota watching people in mall parking lots struggle with kids, store merchandise bags, backpacks, strollers, grocery carts, etc., while fumbling for their keys to unlock the manual sliding door. Those customers were screaming, "Give me a damned automatic door opener!" without saying a word. There are literally thousands of examples of this type of thing. Key point: Toyota didn't add cupholders because the competition was. The added them because their customers needed them!

A word about bundling here. Sometimes companies want to incentivize purchases this way. It's a way to empty your warehouse of unsold products but it is NOT usually very customer centered. In effect, you are forcing them to buy up your unused merchandise. If you must do so, just make sure you are clear on why you are doing it.

For the record, if I want to buy instant Cinnamon Maple Oatmeal, I don't want to be forced into buying the 'variety pack' and having to buy Apple Raisin just to get what I want! It's gross!

Bottom line here is stay true to your customers' *real* needs, expressed or not, and try to resist products or features that your competition may be adding that have no actual appeal to them. Your accountants will love you for it, too!

Industry-Specific Notes

Healthcare: Acute

Outside of manufacturing, I know of no industry that has embraced lean more than the healthcare domain. There are many reasons for this, but one must be the insanely inefficient nature of the delivery systems currently in place. There is so much waste that it's intimidating and sometimes mind boggling! As such, it can be difficult to even know where to start! My own experience in this realm has taught me to start, as Taiichi Ohno put it, "In the areas of greatest need". But where is that? Ultimately, it's all about flow!

Think about it, we have institutionalized one of the biggest forms of waste: waiting. Waiting rooms are in and of themselves conspicuous *artifacts of waste.* And yet, we have even designed and built them INTO our shiny new buildings. Why do we have them? This line of thinking may seem crazy. I mean, everybody knows, including the patient, that waiting is part of the process, right? But why? If patients show up carrying their knitting stuff, pay attention.

For the record, I am NOT advocating eliminating waiting rooms for guests and family standing by until their loved ones have completed their procedures, tests, etc. I AM, however, advocating asking the question of why the patients themselves have to move from waiting room to waiting room to waiting room before they receive the value they came for.

Consider, too, that waiting rooms do NOT produce revenue! If that same space can be made available for more treatment areas, etc., you will have a benefit double whammy! I mean, where would YOU or your loved ones prefer to go, a place of chaos and confusion or one of efficient smooth flow? Fortunately, good work has been going on and many great books, articles, etc., are out there on this topic. See Chapter 13 for a partial list.

While the Emergency Department (ED) is often the focus of many improvement projects, it may also lead to an early demise of your lean journey. EDs are notorious for being an improvement quagmire. Because the ED is an extraordinarily complex intersection of many value streams, it isn't the best place to start, in my view. It is even hard for the patient to comprehend. I generally discourage my clients from diving into the ED prematurely.

The nature of the work of ED is so fluid and so full of variation and shifting priorities on a minute-by-minute basis that it is something of a moving target. To the outsider, and this includes patients and their families, emergency rooms seem like chaotic and frenzied places. It reminds me of the stock exchange trading floor. To many patients, it just isn't worth the wait, so they just leave.

They would rather go back home or somewhere else than sit there getting sicker and sicker. They may resent it, too. They came there because they expected you to care for them, not ignore them for eight hours or more! Not a good business model for sure. If you do choose to work in the ED, look at your "Left Without Being Seen" (LWBS) and elopement data. There may be trends there worth studying. Word of advice: start small!

So, instead of starting in the ED, I have learned that it is better to focus first on a single strand of the knot rather than try to take it on all at once.

For example, the lab or imaging value streams may be a better place to launch your lean intervention. Yes, they will wrap around ED processes, but it will be easier to follow one thread at a time rather than try to tackle everything at once.

Some common starting points for lean entry can also be in non-clinical departments such as revenue stream (where improvements can yield significant financial gains), facilities, HR, supply chain, registration, biomed, EVS/housekeeping, etc. Given a choice, I tend to favor using 5S/6S improvements in these types of functions as a beachhead.

For reasons discussed earlier, 5S will create a positive buzz around the organization and will result in very conspicuous improvements relatively quickly. Starting out on such a footing will gain you some momentum for your lean agenda. It will also diminish some of the inherent resistance by getting some quick wins under your belt. Having solid improvements made in such highly visible ways provides you with a reservoir of goodwill from which to draw on later as you dive into much more complex and potentially controversial areas.

Another option is to start in outpatient/same day surgery (SDS), imaging, or the GI lab. These are quasi-production lines. Viewed as such, much of the good work in manufacturing is easily translated into these value streams. In fact, many of the lean traditional tools and concepts apply very neatly here.

Another good place to start is by isolating your key value streams. Remember that, to your patients, value flows horizontally across the enterprise. That is, they see your hospital as a single, integrated entity. If they only knew! Therefore, when they get billed, they can easily get confused by a highly segmented statement or multiple bills reflecting charges for ER, lab, imaging, providers, supplies, etc. Each area has its own respective silo.

Try to answer this question, "How much does a hip replacement cost?" Seems like a straightforward question, doesn't it? Any other commodity we purchase has a price. Price is a known value upfront and is a key factor in a purchase decision. So, why not hospital services? Your customers (we call them patients) don't want to hear, "Well, it depends".

As an executive leader in the healthcare world, you will need a well-grounded and experienced lean consultant/partner by your side. They can help you avoid many of the pitfalls that can derail your best intentions.

Please allow me to contradict myself here. In the case of acute healthcare, I would say that it does help to have a consultant with legitimate hospital experience. As I mentioned earlier, it is frequently preferable to have an external consultant with little or no specific experience in your world serving as 'outside eyes'. But here, not so much. This is a territory that takes years to even begin to comprehend. Healthcare is an incredibly unique world with very distinctive and unique challenges.

I suggest you engage your lean partner to conduct a high level, 'Executive VSA (Value Stream Analysis), early on. It can serve as a strategic blueprint for your overall lean reconstruction efforts. Once complete, it will force a dialogue about how to prioritize and sequence your kaizen activities, resulting in a comprehensive and strategic improvement plan. As mentioned previously, "Sometimes you have to go slow to go fast". True, this.

Even a simple question like, "who is the customer?" can devolve into a heated conversation. Therefore, you may want to find somebody already familiar with your environment, challenges, available resources, etc. You may also want to assess the readiness of the staff.

All of us have a short list of those folks that are always eager to try something new. Bless them. This should also factor into your equation about when, where and how to start. So, take a deep breath and choose your starting place, or model cell, wisely. Chances are if you start well, you will end well. Keep a long view and be clear about your ultimate goals.

Healthcare: Ambulatory

While still in the healthcare domain, ambulatory settings are typically easier to improve. They tend to be smaller and easier to get your arms around. Here, I would recommend starting by observing the flow of patients, providers, staff and information.

Your lean partner/consultant will probably recommend that you produce a spaghetti diagram from those observations. You may want to look at the way your physical plant is laid out from it. Frequently, this will make your improvement needs obvious. Does the work flow in linear fashion or is the patient flow more herky-jerky around the place? If so, does it have to be that way?

A harder place, but a very worthwhile place to start is in your revenue stream. There are huge potential savings and increased earnings to be gained from untangling the flow of money to and from the clinic. Start timing the processes from billing to reimbursement (if any), for example. Prepare to be shocked by your 'first pass yield'. This is how often a process achieves its desired result on the first try. It might be at or near zero.

The insurance industry, as everybody knows, is its own incredible mess. I have to admit that, for me at least, it is still very much of a black hole! But, while you can't control them, there are lots of things you can do on your end that will result in significant gains for you from your own internal process improvement work.

Are all your treatment/exam rooms standardized? As easy as it sounds, this can surface a host of issues related to individual preferences, parochial territorialism, hoarding, etc. Nevertheless, by standardizing the exam rooms, you can achieve surprising improvements in productivity, waste reduction and even morale. A perfect place to introduce 5S.

Remember that RNs are not taught hunting and gathering in nursing school. Yet, this process is a quite common, if not constant and time-consuming process that occurs all day, every day. Ask them what they routinely hunt for. Ask them a simple question, "What bugs you?" You may be surprised by their answers.

This is also a big issue in the acute setting referenced above. Again, 5S/6S can be a great place to start. From that process you will uncover where excess supplies and even obsolete equipment has been hiding (or hidden).

Note: Hoarding is a result of staff wanting to make sure that they have what they need when they need it. Crazy concept isn't it? Hoarding is a symptom of a larger issue, though. Your consultant will help expose where stockpiles of materials may have been hidden but more importantly, why they have been hidden and who hid them.

Remember, nobody goes to work with the express intent of doing a bad job. There are very good people trying to work in bad processes! Make it easy for them to do the right thing and nearly impossible to do the wrong thing.

Construction

Construction is by its very nature a project management business. Many Project Managers (PMs) are formally trained in that discipline. They are NOT, however, trained in *process* improvement methodology. Put somewhat cynically, a project manager can build the wrong thing on time and within budget. Worse, they can build something for which there is no customer.

I say this to split the hairs between PMs and lean consultants. The latter will primarily focus on the *how* of what is built vs. the *what*. For example,

I consulted with a large developer of residential properties. We are talking about huge projects encompassing hundreds of acres and thousands of homes in phases and tracts here. As in any other discipline, it's easy to accumulate waste in such an endeavor as this. I'll use one example showing the waste of 'rework'.

Story Time: *Planned Rework? What?*

A little background: When building a new development, many jurisdictions require that certain infrastructure be completed first, before the actual home sites can be developed. This includes obvious things like lights, utilities, sewers, streets, etc. Typically, once that construction is complete and approved, only then can the actual homes be built.

An all-but-certain outcome of this process is the gradual destruction of the roads, curbs and sidewalks once the actual home building part begins. Those sites must be breached by heavy equipment (e.g., cement mixers, forklifts, backhoes, tractors and the like) throughout the building process. Once the homes are completed, construction companies must repair the damage done to the new home site that occurred during its construction. It is considered an inevitable part of the process.

One example: One such development had a rather large budget line item devoted to repair and replacement of damaged sidewalks and curbs before the homeowner could occupy their new homes. I studied the issue and realized that damage was occurring since the sidewalk was often 4–6 inches higher than the dirt driveway that they needed to use to access the site. Big equipment would roll over the sidewalk and crush the edges of the sidewalk until they had to be replaced before the driveway could be poured and the home could be released for sale.

Experiment #1: Put gravel along the inside edge of the sidewalk facing the dirt driveway thus offering a tapered ramp of sorts and protecting the vulnerable, exposed sidewalk edges. This was made even more useful since they needed the gravel to build the driveway anyway. So, why not put it in place a little earlier in the process? This was so effective that it became a standard practice going forward and the cost of this specific type of repair was reduced to near zero.

Experiment #2: To try something else regarding the same problem, we used strong steel pipe just inside the sidewalk that would be slightly taller than the sidewalk concrete. When the equipment rolled over it, it protected the unreinforced edges. It also worked perfectly but was abandoned, as it required pulling the pipe back out, which necessitated a new, if less drastic, form of rework.

So, yes, the construction industry builds things. Lean is a way to ensure that waste is identified and eliminated at every step along the way. There is enormous opportunity in the realm of materials and supplies as well as scheduling and inclement weather workarounds. Many more examples can be found as lean has entered the construction world.

As an executive in this arena, I recommend that you find an experienced lean consultant and pay him/her to observe on a per diem basis for a few days. Depending on what he or she 'sees' during that observation, you will be in a better position to decide if that person is the right consultant for you. Remember: looking is not necessarily seeing. A trained observer knows what to look for and will find things that untrained observers won't.

Law Enforcement

My own experience in this realm was shocking. I was speechless when I saw some of the broken and ancient systems that are still in use. Paper still rules the day in many places. Here are some startling stories. For their sake, no specific PDs will be identified.

Story Time: *In the Jailhouse*

1. A clipboard holding paper that was cut into half-inch strips served as the 'inventory' of arrestees in a jail. One day while I was there, a sudden gust of wind from an open window blew the clipboard off the wall and landed under a desk. The strips were recovered, but the janitor later found one that had been missed. The result was that an arrestee in a holding cell became invisible to their 'system', where he languished until he finally asked, "Hey, does anybody know I'm here?" Seriously. You can't make this stuff up!
2. Another case. Two officers are typically in a patrol car. They deliver an arrestee to the jail, where they start the long and paper-intensive pre-booking/booking process. One does the work while the other sits around drinking coffee waiting. These same officers were in the car

together for the time it took to arrest the guy and drive him to the jail. When the paperwork was complete, one officer, handcuffed to the suspect, would then wait in line for the next available jailer window to open. Think bank lines. At that point, the officer served one single purpose. As an anchor to keep the arrestee from fleeing.

3. A field search of the arrestee was conducted at the point of arrest. Personal property items were placed in a property envelope, documented and then transferred to the jailer. The jailer inventoried and recorded the contents, and then transferred the same items into a new property envelope to go to property control. While each handoff required a sign-off, no sign-off was ever asked of the arrestee. Meanwhile, the suspect, once released from custody, screamed, "Hey, where's my Rolex?" (Funny how many arrestees claim to have Rolexes.) The jurisdiction had no way to prove that there was not a Rolex at booking. Therefore, guess who paid? Solution: Have the arrestee sign the original property envelope, collected at the point of arrest, across the seal of the envelope. Then, when released, all the arrestee had to do was to confirm that his signature was still intact and thus validate that the envelope had not been opened.

Here's a tricky question in the booking process: "Who is the customer?" Normally, the answer has to do with who benefits from the transaction. Does the arrestee qualify? Well, does he benefit from your efforts to be more efficient at locking him up? Hmmm …

OK, well maybe the arrestee isn't the customer. Maybe it's the officer(s)? Maybe. Data revealed that most of the arrests were occurring near the end of the officers' shifts. Digging deeper revealed that the officers timed their arrests whenever possible to end their day at the jail and therefore not to have to return to the field. They knew about how long the booking process would take and leveraged it to their advantage.

This way they improved their chances of getting off on time and making it to their kids' soccer games. Hmmm. They actually figured out how to exploit the inefficiencies of the jail to avoid returning to the field, imagine that.

So, again, who's the customer? To finish the story, it turns out that there were two customers, the beat sergeant who had a stake in keeping officers in the field and the community at large. So sometimes a fairly simple question, "Who's the customer?" can reveal a lot of information.

Lean professionals will help expose these kinds of things and help untangle the mess that years of administrative neglect has created.

Chapter 13

Some Great Resources

Forums and Seminars

The Lean Summit This is a big event every year. It's a great place to meet with a wide assortment of other companies, industries and individuals in every phase of their lean journey. You will learn a lot. If you plan to attend, bring your key leaders with you, and learn together. You'll find details on this and many other seminars and webinars on the Lean Enterprise Institute (LEI) website, www.lean.org.

Consultants

Be really careful here. There are 'consultants' out there that will take you down the wrong path. I have had several contracts where my first step was to undo the damage done by them. When considering using a specific consultant or consulting company, below are a few interview questions to ask.

Trust me on this. Do your due diligence now and save yourself a lot of anguish, disillusionment and money later! If they're any good, chances are that there are a lot of references available for you.

Here are ten specific interview questions for you to consider asking a potential lean consulting partner:

1. ***Is your approach consistent with the Toyota (LEI) methodology? How so? If not, why not?***
2. ***Have you branded anything that is uniquely yours?*** Careful. This can be an indication of a faux lean or Toyota-esque company seeking to develop their own unique 'Brand X' lean product line.

3. ***Tell me about your experience in this industry. How did you get your training?*** **Note**: It is NOT critical that you find a good consultant with experience in your industry, per se. It may help somewhat in the learning curve for your specific organization though. Sometimes it's best to hire someone with a legitimate outsider's perspective. Typically, they will ask more and better questions! My standard answer when asked about how much I know about a specific industry for which I have no experience is, "Nothing, but I don't charge extra for my ignorance".
4. ***Tell me about your staff's experience and specialties.*** In some consulting firms, they have specialists (i.e., executive coaches) as well as the main consultant team that may focus on setting up shop for you; others specialize in specific value streams, etc.
5. ***Who would actually be assigned to work with us day today?*** Watch out for 'bait-and-switch' contracts! Sometimes they will use a 'pitch man' to get you to sign a contract and then later switch you over to the actual consultant team. Danger.
6. ***Describe the objective results you achieved at the organizations you helped so far. How can we go see what you have done?*** Self-explanatory.
7. ***Who of your previous clients can I visit with that had the closest knowledge of your work there?*** 'Go-and-see' is a foundational notion in lean cultures. Ask if the consultant can get you into one or more of the places they have worked. Be ready to offer to do likewise and host some future visitors to your place to help them along their own lean journeys. Remember: *A rising tide raises all boats!*
8. ***Do you offer a certification?*** Kind of a trick question. MOST good consultants do *NOT*! This is often an incentive for you to sign up, but most so called 'certifications' are meaningless in this industry. They don't usually hurt anything but do not base your decision on it. Having said that, some consulting companies will provide a certificate of completion to recognize learning progress. Perfectly appropriate.
9. ***Are you strictly a lean consultant or are you a Lean/Six Sigma consultant?*** **Note**: The industry is moving away from Six Sigma rapidly. Avoid it! Many former Six Sigma practitioners have had to rebrand themselves as they jumped from the Six Sigma Titanic. Collectively, the industry began introducing themselves as a new hybrid called "Lean/Six Sigma" to bridge the gap. Just be careful here. Explore the differences with them deeply.